TRANSCONTINENTAL

An Investigation of Reality

Nine Latin American Artists

**WALTERCIO CALDAS · JUAN DAVILA · EUGENIO DITTBORN · ROBERTO EVANGELISTA
VICTOR GRIPPO · JAC LEIRNER · CILDO MEIRELES · TUNGA · REGINA VATER**

Guy Brett

WITH TEXTS BY THE ARTISTS, LU MENEZES and PAULO VENANCIO FILHO

VERSO

London - New York

(in association with Ikon Gallery, Birmingham and Cornerhouse, Manchester).

First published by Verso, in association with Ikon Gallery,
Birmingham & Cornerhouse, Manchester, 1990.

Verso
UK: 6 Meard Street, London W1V 3HR Tel: 01 437 3546
USA: 29 West 35th Street, New York, NY 10001-2291

Verso is the imprint of New Left Books
A CIP catalogue record for this book is available
from the British Library.

ISBN: 9780860915119

Design: Julian Evans, Lionart Associates, Birmingham
Typeset by Lionart Associates

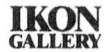

154299744

Contents

We are mixed with each other in ways that most national systems of education have not dreamed of. How to match knowledge in both the arts and the sciences with these integrative realities is, I believe, the issue of the moment as the decade closes.

- Edward Said, The Guardian, Dec 16-17, 1989.

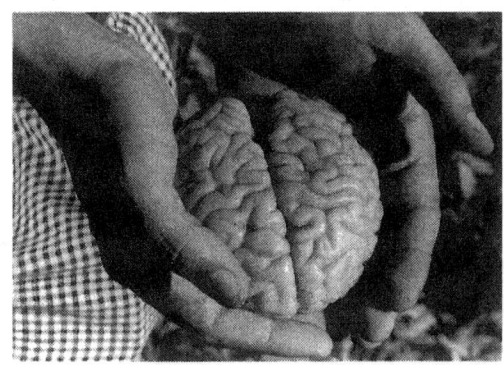

Tunga, still from the video **0 Nervo de Prata (The Silver Nerve)** directed by Arthur Omar and Tunga, Rio de Janeiro 1986.

Preface: assembly

People have begun to talk of a 'boom' in Latin American art such as has existed for some time for Latin American literature, at least for certain writers. A number of 'Latin American' exhibitions of have taken place in museums in Europe and the United States in the past two or three years, including a major survey at the Hayward Gallery, London in 1989. The role which international power politics, money and fashion play in these changes, and how durable they are, could be the subject of a thoughtful analysis (Latin Americans are familiar with booms *and* busts). Up to now, the interest has been mainly in historical art and important contemporary artists are still largely unrepresented in European and North American museums. To make these artists more visible and known must be good, but cultural booms and fashion do not change the fundamental divisions and inequalities in the world. These are expressed, among other things, in differences of cultural infrastructure and therefore in the possibility of producing art.

Another aspect of these inequalities is that the curatorial strategies applied in the Western metropolis, either by choice or necessity, to exhibitions of 'Latin American art' have been different from and much cruder than those applied to European art. Some take the form of the survey, with its inevitable over-simplification and homogenization of another reality (as well as the impossibility of including all artists who could and should be represented under such a strategy). Others perpetuate the myth of the odyssey, a report of the exploration of a far-off unknown land in search of art. Travelling in the other direction, so to speak, was an event like *Margins and Institutions: Art in Chile 1973-1989* (The Showroom, London 1989), where the desire of Chilean avant-garde artists to present their work in Europe necessitated the 'guerilla' tactic of a compressed, urgent 'briefing' on slides and video. For different reasons, such exhibitions have tended to emphasise a polarized relationship between 'there' and 'here', between 'they' and 'we'. The individual artists themselves tend to become homogenised as a group from 'over there': the latest novelty, the latest instalment in our cultural consumption patterns which we might pride ourselves were becoming increasingly cosmopolitan. Rather than consumption, a dialogue is needed, a discussion on the effectiveness of a plurality of tactics which exist today.

This book should declare its own limitations. Like the exhibition it is based on, it is not intended to be a survey. In relation to the term 'Latin America', it is obvious that the artists discussed here come from only three of the southernmost countries of the continent. Their work belongs to an international urban practice of art and can therefore be more easily translated to a European gallery than some other kinds of work which would need a different preparation if the context and force of its working was not to be lost. But this is not an apology. The work of these artists bursts on the scene in the form of powerful and lucid strategies, new and complex metaphors, in which what is 'local' cannot in fact be separated from what is 'global'.

Even the rather complicated logistical process of assembling the exhibition (assembly of the materials became the assembly of the active components of the metaphor), tended to break down rigid polarities. In the case of Jac Leirner's *Os Cem* ('The Hundreds'), for example, the banknotes had to come from Brazil, their power as signs being related to the reality of hyper-inflation and their graffiti testifying to people's opinions and dreams in those specific conditions. The plastic bags of *Nomes* ('Names'), another work by Jac Leirner, were collected internationally. Similarly, Jac Leirner's concept of the Error is expressed both through Brazilian TV advertising jargon, and through a British equivalent (collected over Christmas 1989 by Ikon Gallery for Jac Leirner to work on).

A similar process took place with each artist. In Victor Grippo's *Analogy*, some items had to come from Argentina, but potatoes and cheap electrical components (and this is part of the meaning) would be available almost anywhere. Tunga's magnets came from a factory in Sheffield and were the waste of British imports from Brazil! Cildo Meireles' coins in *How to Build Cathedrals* are English 1p pieces, alluding here to an oppressive social reality such as that instituted in the 17th century by the Jesuit missions in southern Brazil. Some of the feathers in Regina Vater's and Roberto Evangelista's *Nika Uiicana* ('Union of People') installation were moulted by tropical birds languishing in Twycross Zoo, near Birmingham. Waltercio Caldas' granite pieces were shipped over, but *Mirror with Light* made up here. Juan Davila, who lives in Australia, painted three seven-metre long paintings specially for the show, partly to cut transport costs, but mainly to 'answer back', to make a critical response to certain aspects of 'British' culture, including Western views of Latin America.

With Eugenio Dittborn's Airmail Paintings, no special logistical effort of linking needed to be made, since by displaying the envelopes they are sent in, they incorporate into their artistic structure their own process of travelling. Their passage through the post becomes part of a whole meditation on closeness and distance, on 'periphery' and 'centre', on contact and abyss.

If these components of the material language are a mixture of the 'site-specific' and planetary, this grouping of artists as a whole represents a meeting of the topical and the abstract. The word 'abstract' perhaps needs a redefinition today, it needs to be reclaimed from its stereotypical association with so-called esoteric or 'high' culture. Abstraction represents a kind of spatial and temporal freedom, an elasticity of language beyond all fixing, a potentiality of meaning. In one sense, therefore, the exhibition and this book are about the relation, the tension, between the abstract/void and the contingent, localised, historical, urgent and conflicted. During a conversation , Cildo Meireles related to me two childhood memories of growing up in Goîania, a town in central Brazil. One was of the vast space of the countryside, the sight of a human being moving in the extreme, flat distance. The other was one day when his father came home crying; he took Cildo by the hand and led him to a place where a progressive journalist had been shot down outside his newspaper office, by order of the local landlords. People had written a protest on the wall in his own blood ■

Border Crossings

The New York Museum of Modern Art's exhibition *Information* (1970) was one of the very few contemporary survey exhibitions organized by a major Western cultural institution in the last twenty years which included a number of artists from outside Europe or North America. Anyone flicking through the catalogue will find an agitated, discontented personal statement by the Brazilian artist Hélio Oiticica.[1]

He begins by saying "I am not here representing Brazil, or anything else; the ideas of representing, representation, are over." He goes on to describe *Tropicália*, a 1960s movement spanning the arts in Brazil in which he played a leading role, and which attempted to create, as he put it, "a synthetic face-Brazil": a language "which would be ours, characteristic of us, which would stand up against imagetic international pop and op art in which a good many of our artists were submerged." But *Tropicália* in this respect, he admits, was a failure, quickly taken over by commercial and official interests and turned again into easily-consumable images: this time typically 'tropical', Brazilian ones. "To survive Brazil", caught between the international and the stereotypically national - "the country that simply doesn't exist" - Oiticica proposed his own notion of art, where 'life-acts' and 'behaviour' would replace the image as a kind of experimental practice which could be exported anywhere, taken up by others and mix with local cultural possibilities.

Oiticica's imaginative and provocative work will be returned to later. What is especially interesting here is his phrase "the country that simply doesn't exist". For it shows up the simultaneously real and chimerical nature of 'cultural identities'. There is no 'Brazil', he seems to be saying, only a plethora of 'Brazils', of mental images generated by different groups and individuals both inside and outside the country. The images of Latin America as a whole generated in Europe or North America are influenced by distance, by the interests of different specialists, by the media, and by a romantic projection whose vision of Latin America seems to see-saw between paradise and hell. Despite changing emphases, these are relentlessly homogenizing images which cover over the internal distinctions of class and race, region and culture. The result is a polarization (here/there, we/they), rather than the kind of dynamic complexity which would set up comparisons with our own culture. Where do 'our' externally-constructed images meet or miss 'their' internally-constructed ones which are continually, and often violently, engaged in 'inventing' the nation itself, as the sociologist José Jaoquin Brunner has described for his own country, Chile:

In Chile, rather than a national identity we have a culture of a plurality of identities. Rather than being a nation, we are a territory of conflicting national images, an idealization of projects for nationhood, a set of competing utopias. We are a country of pedagogues and ideologues, of jurists and communicators, of legislators and intellectuals, where each group, party, school or sect dreams of imposing its own 'country model'. We are a country that has scarcely been made material reality, but has been baptized a thousand times with a name rather than actively transformed by hand or machine; a country more sacramental than productive, constructed of gestures and rituals rather than productive enterprises and tools.[2]

Part of the complexity is that, if the countries of Latin America still suffer from a colonial, or neo-colonial, relationship with Europe and North America, they are also partly internally constituted by the same myths and attitudes (for example, by the mentality of the settler, or of the patriarchal authority, by myths of the noble savage, and so on).[3]

The centres of power have always assumed the right to define and explain the rest of the world. The West assumes, consciously or unconsciously, that it is 'the measure of all things'. (I heard this phrase used most recently by an East German student who complained on British TV that the Western media's coverage of the destruction of the Berlin Wall gave the impression that the West was virtually 'tutoring' the changes in his country: "They talk as if we're just following the path they set forty years ago, as if all we want is what they already have. They can't understand that maybe there's something else, something of our own", he said). These assumptions lead to an unresolvable dilemma when it comes to the presentation of art by Latin Americans in the metropolitan centres. It becomes a complex play of positive and negative. If these presentations stress cultural similarity, they are positive in the sense that they acknowledge that Latin America is part of the mainstream of modern culture, but raise the danger of assimilating the work to a bland 'international art' which makes nothing of the context from which the art comes, and especially the fundamental gap between the living standards of the First and Third worlds. If on the other hand, the presentation stresses difference, it acknowledges that Latin America has a history, cultures, and present conditions different from those of Europe, but raises the danger of defining those differences in telluric, folkloric, essentialist terms. Both sets of alternatives lead inevitably to separate, restrictive categories for the artists. They limit their freedom to concern themselves with any matter whatsoever. No European artists are asked that their work give proof of their 'European identity', but this is always the first thing expected of a Latin American. This restrictive categorization is so powerful, and the assumption of Eurocentricity so implacable, that it often hardly matters if the response of the West is to praise or condemn.

Two recent events in major European museums can serve as an example. In the first, *Magiciens de la Terre* at the Centre Pompidou and La Villette in Paris (1989), which billed itself as "the first global exhibition of contemporary art", the curator Jean-Hubert Martin expressed himself as "disappointed" to discover that Latin Americans have "Western" art networks like ours, with galleries, museums, etc., and that they read *Artforum*. He expected to find something totally different and 'other' which, in his words, would "renew our vision, rejuvenate our interest".[4] He therefore almost completely missed what was in fact of real interest. Later in the same year, the Stedelijk Museum in Amsterdam mounted an exhibition of twelve artists from Argentina, Uruguay, Chile and Brazil. Here, in an apparent inversion, the curator Dorine Mignot praised Latin American artists for their appreciation of the German Anselm Kiefer's work. She actually began her catalogue essay by talking about Kiefer, about the "deep sigh of acknowledgment" which his "genius and unequalled brilliance" had elicited from Brazilian artists when it was shown at the São Paulo Biennale in 1987.[5]

It obviously would not have fitted her mental image of Latin America as somehow deprived to know that Kiefer's work was received critically in Brazil as anywhere else, and that there were also those who were not too impressed by it and considered that possibly more advanced work was being produced in Brazil itself.

◆

Is there the possibility of a 'third way' which goes beyond these alternatives of homogenization and polarization and all that they entail? Is there a more sophisticated model that takes into account the movements and journeys of artists themselves, or the common patterns that arise in attitudes towards experimental art? Is it possible to speak of the meeting and clashing of cultures both in terms of profound differences - and therefore of inevitable misunderstandings - and also in terms of the creation of non-essentialist, multiple identities? Perhaps the best place to seek answers to such questions is on one of today's actual borderlines which is genuinely between two cultures, such as the Mexican-American border. There exists a tradition of acute analysis of the differences between the worlds of 'Latin' and 'Anglo' culture, which would include Octavio Paz's famous book *The Labyrinth of Solitude*, written in the '50s, and the contemporary work of the Border Arts Workshop, a collective of artists, writers and performers based between Tijuana (Mexico) and San Diego (California).

Members of the Border Arts Workshop are concerned with the 'border' as a many-faceted reality or experience: political, legal, economic, cultural, linguistic - as it exists for the undocumented Mexican worker as much as for the Latino or Anglo intellectual. In a recent issue of *Third Text*, Coco Fusco asked Guillermo Gómez-Peña and Emily Hicks, BAW members, about their use of both languages (Spanish and English) in their performances. What were the points of friction or tension in moving from one to the other? Coco Fusco quoted the Cuban writer Edmundo Desnoes as saying that he "perceived the Anglo use of language as an instrument for acquiring things, with an objective". For Desnoes, "the quintessential space for discursive exchange in an Anglo context would be the [shopping] mall." On the other hand he conceived of Spanish as a language in which people realize themselves in the act of speaking, with the plaza as its quintessential space. Guillermo Gómez-Peña made a very interesting reply:

> There are innumerable misconceptions related to the use of language in the border. I
> think that these misconceptions generate mistrust from one group to the other. The
> Mexicans have traditionally been seen as extremely oral; and the Chicanos, having a
> culture of resistance and not a culture of affirmation like the Mexicans, have developed
> an extremely minimal, direct and confrontational way of relating intellectually. Right
> there you have two modes of utilizing language that generate incredible mistrust. The
> Mexican is seen as flowery, as talkative. And the Mexican perceives the Chicano as rude
> and as too direct. Another opposition that we find generates a lot of tensions and
> problems is that California is extremely anti-intellectual, with all the clichés you want to
> name - California is an outdoors culture, an easygoing culture. There is a basic distrust
> of cultures that use language as intellectual enquiry and as pleasure - the whole notion
> of conversation as pleasure, as dialogue, as intellectual enquiry, as a social event, as

ritual, are notions that are very foreign to Californians. When Californians and Mexicans try to sit at the same table, it's very, very difficult to communicate. For the Mexicans, the language has extreme connotations of plasticity, of texture, of sensuality and communication. Whereas for the Californian, it's very pragmatic.

...the pragmatic view is a very foreign notion to us. For us there is a ludic element. There is a mystical element, there is a whole level of imagination; language for the sake of imagining, of inventing, of playing. All these elements that exist in Mexican art and literature are not found on this side of the border. And the border artist has to walk on these bridges very often.[6]

Gómez-Peña's remarks raise poignant questions about possible futures. Is the world to drift more and more towards the 'the language of the mall' as the global market, the media and consumerism infiltrate into every society and every cultural tradition? Or will there be some new kind of synthesis, maybe not the orderly one once imagined by Antonio Gramsci, in which the "good points" of every "national character" would be fused together, but something more chaotic? This brings one back again to questions of power, and of resistance.

◆

Further on in the same *Third Text* interview, Gómez-Peña describes himself as "the child of the ultimate Mexican crisis. Of financial, ecological, intellectual culture. My experience is one of absolute syncretism."[7] The word 'crisis' is one which continually comes up in discussions of the work of Latin American artists, used both by the artists themselves and by critics. Certainly the work of the nine artists recorded here could be seen in terms of a response to crisis - completely differently conceived and staged by each person. At one level everyone knows what this crisis means (it has become a daily shock for every newspaper reader). At the specific level of art, the concept of crisis can be seen as a powerful energizing force and an agent for opening up the 'models' so long used in the West to describe non-European modernism: as exotic, imitative, provincial, and so on. Instead we see an intensification, a 'bringing to crisis' of issues which affect us also, however much they may be disguised by affluence. When Gómez-Peña refers to the 'ultimate' Mexican crisis, he hints that these tensions have a long history.

The "ecological culture" could refer not only to the most well-known features of the global crisis, but to other shared experiences which have the force of the most powerful paradoxes. For example, on the one hand the sensation, often childhood memories, of the vastness of Latin American geography and the richness of nature; on the other, the daily shocks of discovering the finite nature of these resources, and witnessing a growing socio-spatial irrationality where the majority of the population is crowded into urban slums, leaving huge barren hinterlands.[8] In a sense these paradoxes have also a cultural history. In his imaginative book *Del Espacio de Aca* ('About Space Over Here'), written as a study of Eugenio Dittborn's work, Ronald Kay speculated that there had been a kind of mismatch, historically, between the Latin American landscape and the European models used to depict it. Painting had no time, according to Kay, to form another tradition in the New World before it was supplanted by photography, whose images corresponded to a European level of industrialization and urbanization. They therefore clashed with the 'backward' state of Latin America.[9]

Brazil offers one of the great world examples of human actions vis-à-vis the richness of nature, and the clash of attitudes and values. While for a long time the size of the country and the wealth of natural resources[10] seemed to allow an attitude of endlessly taking (mainly by, or for the benefit of, foreign countries), recent events have shown the multiple consequences of the philosophy of dominating nature. Now, as the forests are being destroyed to further the economic ambitions of transnational companies, and Western science has only just begun to test the flora of those forests for their medicinal properties, it is revealed that Indian peoples of the Amazon have long had the most detailed knowledge of tropical sicknesses and how to treat them (the Mêbêngôkre of Paré State, for example, classify over 150 types of diarrhoea/dysentery and the specific plant remedies for each one)[11]. Brazilian Indian populations have declined from about eight million at the time of the first European contact, to less than 200,000 today.

The "financial culture" obviously refers specifically to the huge external debts which dominate the economies of most Latin American countries, and confirm their dependency on the rich nations, especially the United States. Internally, it could describe the experience of hyper-inflation which is obliquely referred to by Jac Leirner's work *Os Cem*. She refers to it both in its material, factual sense, and as a subjective experience for the ordinary population. Many writers have proposed in one form or another a Latin American 'subject' faced by overwhelming contradictions: caught in a cycle between economic booms and busts, between civilian and military rule, between socialist experiments and right-wing tyrannies—"devastating experiences", as José Jaoquin Brunner has put it, "where the greatest hope is mixed with the greatest dread."[12]

What of "intellectual culture", Guillermo Gómez-Peña's third category of crisis? Here it should go without saying that the Latin American intelligentsia have an absolutely modern and international culture, and that new ideas circulate as readily, or more readily, than in Europe. But one of the great differences from most parts of Europe is that it would be hard to imagine a Latin American intellectual working without an awareness of the mass of people. He or she can hardly help being aware of this majority in two of its guises: first as a creative force, a popular or vernacular culture which has been continually re-inventing itself through the centuries of conquest, colonialism, immigration and partial modernization; and second, in its actual conditions of life, its impoverishment, its daily survival struggle, and its marginality to, and often terrorization by, the official order. The relationship between 'fine art' and 'popular culture' is one of the most fascinating questions in the history of art. It goes to the heart of every hierarchical social system; a process of 'revitalization' of fine art by the popular, or 'transformation' of the popular by the erudite whose workings are very complex. In Latin America this relationship still apparently remains an 'open question' in the sense that intellectuals can assign to popular culture the leading role, and the vitality to throw intellectual life into crisis. To quote again from Gómez-Peña's illuminating description:

> Many of the so-called post-modern techniques in the arts, like quoting, borrowed imagery, pastiche, juxtapositions of image and text, and recycling of historical imagery, had taken place in Mexican art, even in popular art, way before post-modernism was coined. It has to do with the fact that Latin America is such a syncretic, eccentric, disjointed fusion of European, Amerindian and Afro-Caribbean culture. This fusion has created a kind of multicentric perspective in Latin American culture that allows for narrative, for spiral thinking, for violent juxtapositions, that take place in the world, in society. The artists and writers observe them and later write about them.[13]

"The culture is one of a multiplicity of times, in which the pre-Columbian and the contemporary exist shoulder to shoulder." When Gómez-Peña describes his experience as one of "absolute syncretism", he implies that these time-gulfs span every sphere of activity: economic, technological, political, cultural.

Traditions that still exist in Latin America are mostly dead in Europe: the story-teller, the popular poet, festive days, true festivity - a loss which European poets, from Baudelaire and Rimbaud to Pasolini, have been lamenting in one form or another. But this is not, once again, to posit a folkloric Latin America against a post-industrial Europe. We might in any case be entering a very different situation if, on the one hand, European thinkers have never been reconciled to this loss, while on the other, countries of the so-called Third World are increasingly experiencing the conditions which in Europe have changed communal forms of culture. Again, a polarization is unimaginative.

If one were to chronicle the history of revolt in Latin America, from the early rebellions of indigenous groups which continued long after the Conquest (including religious movements), through all forms of trade union organization and popular grass-roots movements (to participate in which is to risk one's life - right up until today), one would have an endless list testifying to the immense weight of patriarchal culture. Each revolt has been an attempt to set checks on authoritarian power. In fact today many grass-roots movements have appeared because of a complete loss of faith in the willingness or ability of governments to do anything about major problems. The unofficial energy and imagination of these initiatives is the inverse image of official inertia: for example, the Brazilian rubber-tappers union in the Amazon (led by the activist Chico Mendes who was later murdered), which was formed to fight for a just and constructive future for the rain forests and their inhabitants; the *Madres de la Plaza Mayor* in Buenos Aires who demand justice for their disappeared relatives; the *Asamblea de Barrios* in Mexico City which arose out of the government's failure to deal with the housing problem after the 1986 earthquake; the *Arpilleristas*, women who make protest pictures out of patchwork in the slums of Santiago, Chile; or very recently, the extraordinary movement for poetry taking place in the midst of the appalling violence perpetrated in Medellin, Colombia, by the drug barons (for which the United States must ultimately be held responsible), poetry readings which draw audiences of 6000 people. One of the most remarkable things is that people's isolation (geographical in the case of the rubber-tappers, domestic/economic in the case of poor

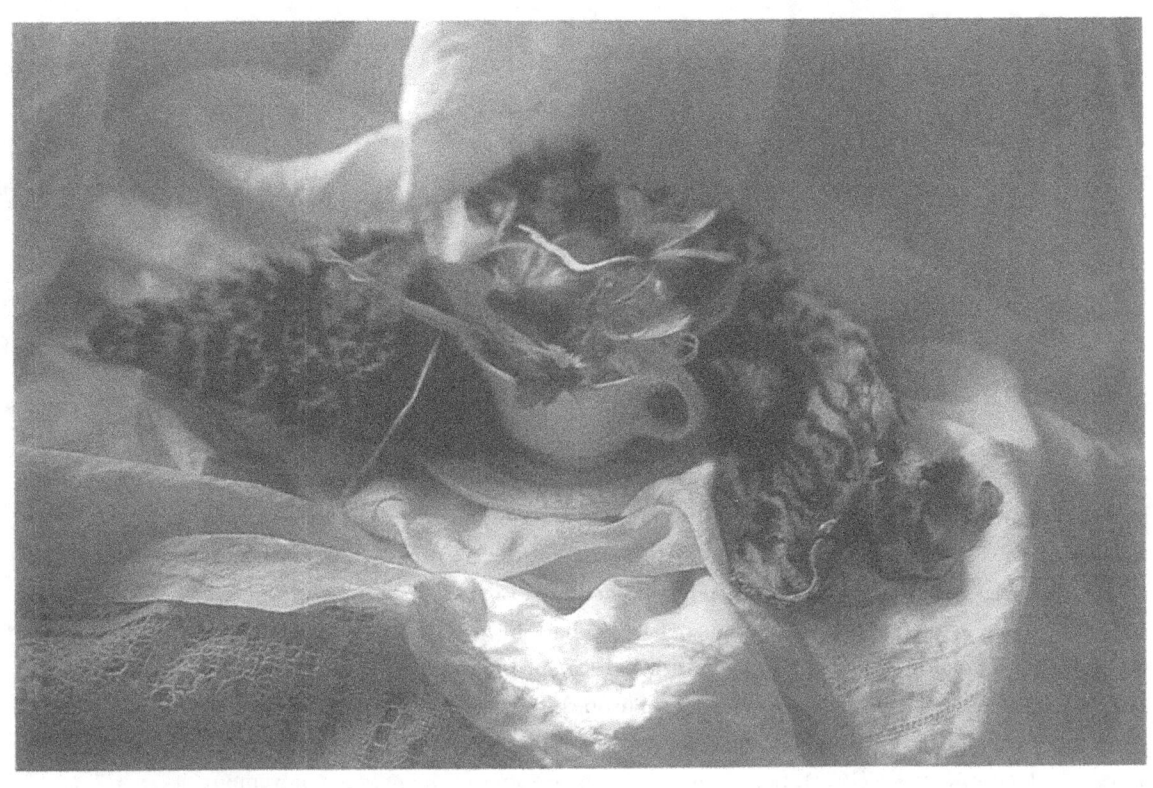

Regina Vater, **Nature Morte** 1989.
Cibachrome print.

women) has not deterred them from organizing.

To outline a certain number of common experiences, made virtually inseparable from one another and intensified by the condition of crisis, is not to say that they necessarily appear directly in any artist's work. It is not so much a question of superficial images as of underlying tensions, forces, relationships, which can be there in the artist who investigates current imagery as well as in the Morandi-type of artist who seems to withdraw from the historical moment. 'Geography' and 'popular culture' have been two sources of energy by which avant-garde movements in Latin America have swept beyond official and academic norms, whose codes and protocols are based on European Beaux-Arts models. This process is brilliantly exemplified in Oswald de Andrade's writings, especially *Pau-Brasil Poetry* (1924) and *Anthropofagic Manifesto* (1928), two of the earliest expressions of the modern movement in Brazil which remain extraordinarily pertinent in 'post-modern' times. Experimental in language, decolonized in spirit, they are a complex "Who am I?" asked by a Brazilian man in the 1920s, a kind of inventory of cultural and historical traces. Anthropofagy (cannibalism) was de Andrade's provocative term for Brazil's absorption of heterogeneous cultures. In his texts, 'erudition' - the orderly range of European academic subjects - is swallowed, enveloped, stretched and exploded in Brazilian conditions:

> Down with bureaucracy, the erudite practice of life. Engineers instead of jurists, lost like Chinamen in the genealogy of ideas.
> Language free of archaisms, free of erudition. Natural and neological. The millionfold contribution of error. How we speak. How we are.[14]

◆

In an essay on Dittborn's work, the Chilean critic Adriana Valdes has provided a succinct summary of the avant-garde artist's situation, which she describes as based on two sorts of tension between 'centre' and 'periphery':

> The first and most obvious, that of...Chile (or the whole of Latin America) as 'peripheral' in relation to the United States and Europe....The second sort of tensions has to do with 'centre' and 'periphery' within peripheral societies: the gaps existing

between the minorities that produce this sort of art and the immense extensions - social (human) and natural - untouched by such artistic activity and indeed even by the social organization that makes it possible or conceivable.[15]

The avant-garde is in one sense an international research community, and the Latin American artist has had to assert his or her place in it by various tactics: travel, residence in the United States or Europe, or other forms of exchanging work and ideas which do not depend on a developed cultural infrastructure. Eugenio Dittborn's Airmail Paintings clearly represent such a tactic. Both in their content and their form, they mediate between, and meditate on, these two isolations, two gulfs, that Valdes describes.[16]

In Brazil the legacy of the modernist experiment which began with Oswald de Andrade's Modern Art Week in São Paulo in 1922 was only handed on by the slenderest thread to be rediscovered during the next cultural explosion of the 1950s, which produced the Neo-concrete movement in the visual arts, Brazil's modern architecture boom, Bossa Nova in music, and the beginnings of Cinema Novo. It was virtually impossible to be an artist unless one had private means. Because of the lack of a cultural infrastructure, outside a few ossified official institutions, one should not speak of a history of art but of "a struggle for the possibility of art" [Paulo Venâncio Filho[17]]. Yet the gradual creation of an infrastructure for art from the late '60s on was extremely problematic in Brazil. The experimental art of the '60s had broken with institutional frameworks in various radical ways which linked up with movements in Europe, re-inventing them in Brazilian conditions. When, therefore, with the arrival of Pop art in the late '60s, art galleries and an art market began to establish themselves in Brazil, two antagonistic tendencies appeared. One favoured integrating Brazil into the international art system as it currently operates, adopting the smooth kind of managerial organization which packages art and addresses its audience as consumers. The other, articulated in magazines like *Malasartes* (1970s) and *A Parte do Fogo* (1980), was highly critical of the international institution of art and linked the growth of an art world in Brazil with conservatism and social privilege. These latter writers and artists looked for alternative ways to act and communicate. The conflict continues today, but in an atmosphere, it must be said, where every infrastructural institution is fragile enough.

And the doors of European and American museums remained on the whole closed to Latin Americans. Art histories in the powerful countries, for the visual arts at least, have

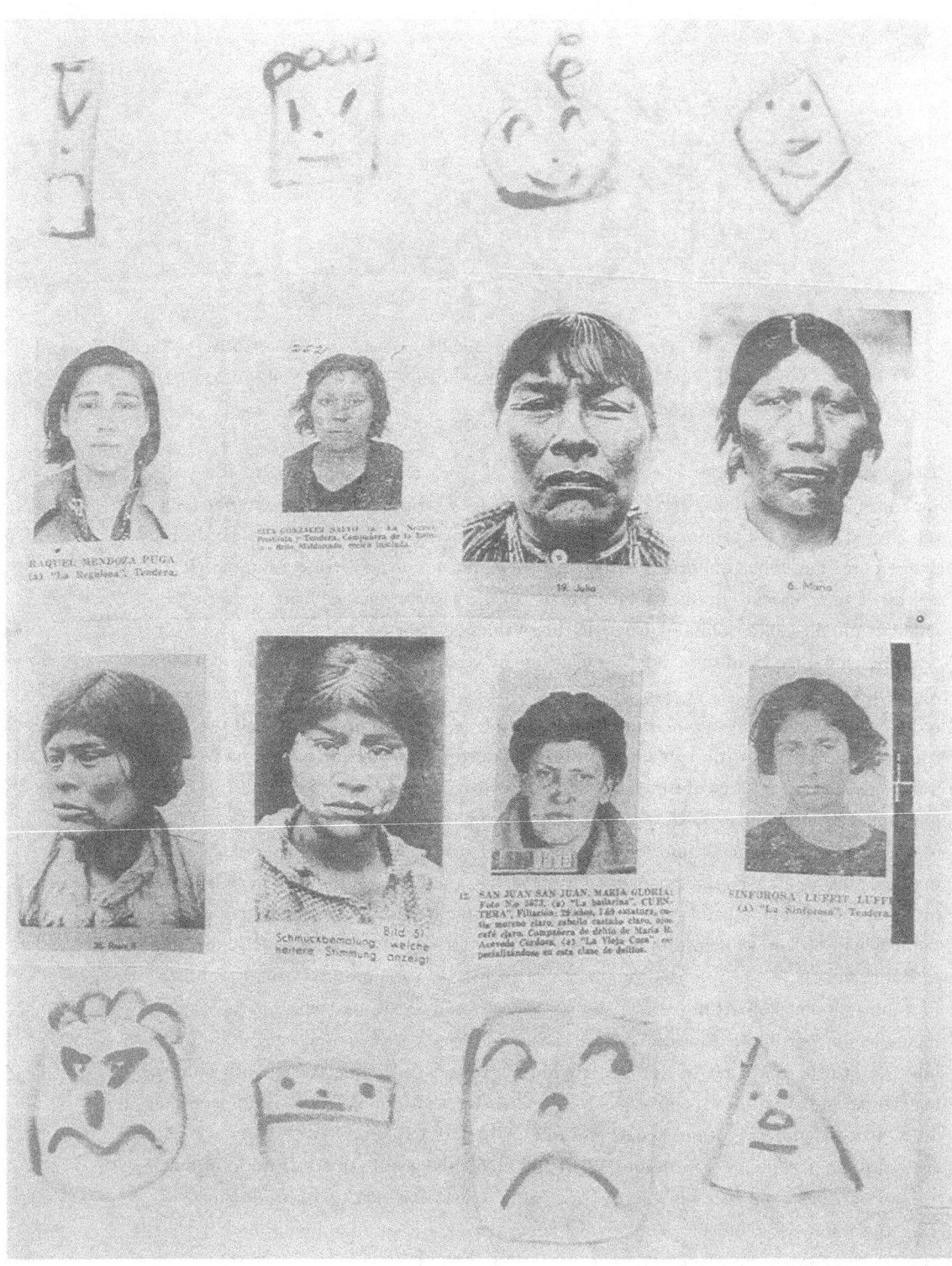

Eugenio Dittborn, **Airmail Painting N° 70, V History of the Human Face (London Camino)** 1989.
(detail of triptych) Painting and photosilkscreen on three fragments of non-woven fabric.

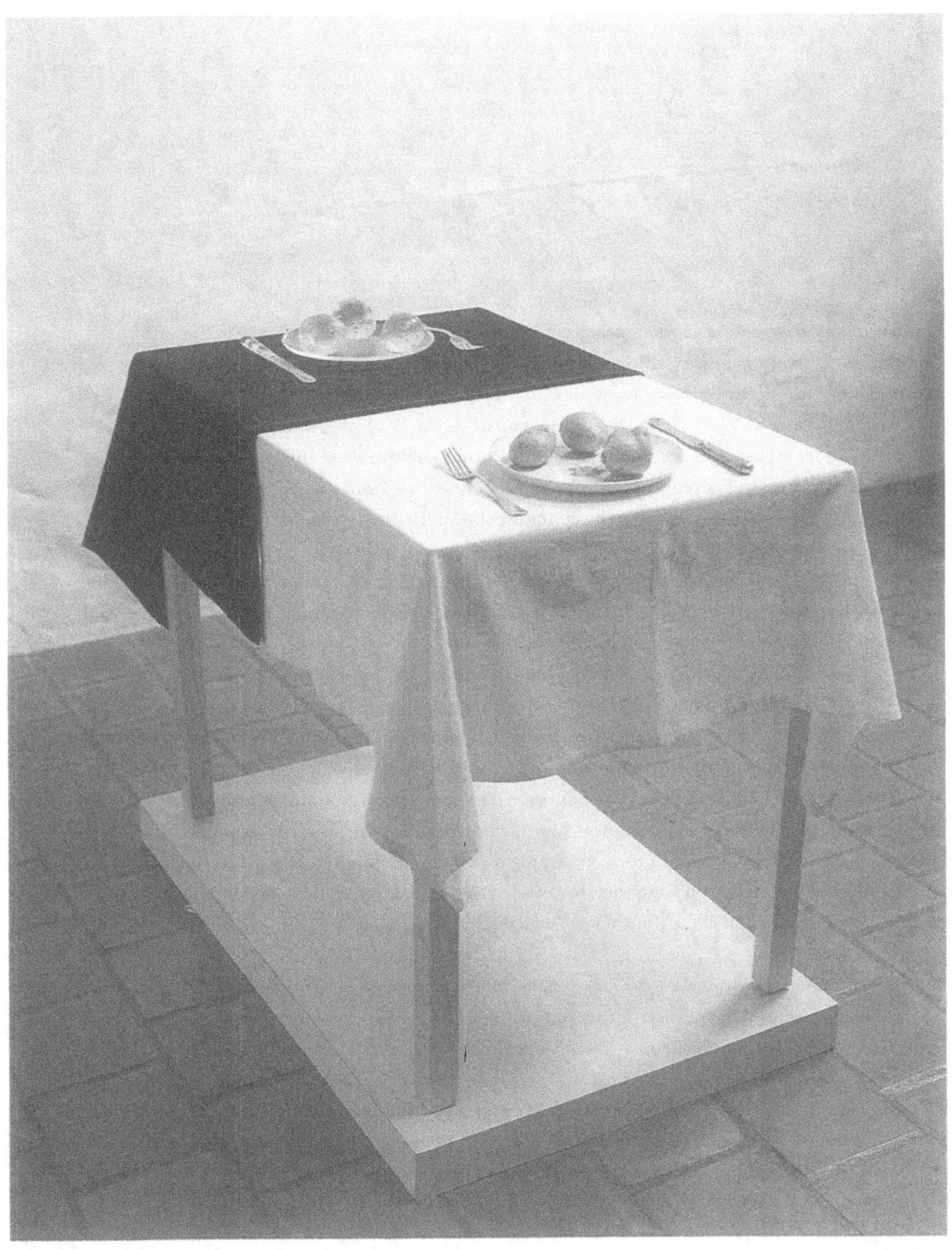

Victor Grippo, **Analogy IV** 1972.
Collection Jorge and Marion Helft, Buenos Aires.

constructed all the post-war movements around 'their' artists, establishing a mainstream of familiar, successful images to which anything else is made to look peripheral, or less successful, even if, in historical terms, it appeared first. The dispute over 'who did it first' only has importance as a way of challenging the system's chauvinistic over-exposure of some artists and under-exposure of others. Otherwise, such issues only disguise the fact that ideas are 'in the air' and are given an extraordinary richness and diversity of inflections, hybridizations and meanings in different cultural contexts (is United States art any less a hybrid in this sense?). Different international models can have an intense application at different places and times, when the vital element of lived experience dispels any merely academic or colonised mimicry. But the climate has not yet been created for the appreciation of these extremely important distinctions.[18]

In her essays, the Chilean critic Nelly Richard has given an acute analysis both of the reception of avant-garde ideas in 'peripheral' countries (particularly Chile) and the responses to Chilean art in the Western metropolis. Typically there has been a failure of communication. Chilean art either did not meet metropolitan expectations of a 'Third World' culture, or it was considered passé in style. Few understood how an "international model' could be tinkered with and given new meanings and inflections of discourse in different societies than those of Europe."[19] Writing about the reception of Pop art in Brazil in the 60s-70s, Paulo Venâncio Filho says that, while Pop formed one of the base-frames for Brazilian experimentation at the time, it was "structurally problematic":

> What in America was the simple appropriation by the artist of an image previously chosen, designated by consumer society and circulating until its obsolescence, was not viable here. The Brazilian Pop artists were confronted with this limitation: in the impossibility of finding signs abstracted and emptied by consumption, they tried instead to take on the unequal and polarized urban reality of the Brazilian metropolis: its aspirations and its miseries. In this way a residue of affective feeling, an inevitable emotion, persisted in their work: very different to the cynicism and indifference of Pop.[20]

If one was to compare, in the light of this observation, the work of Andy Warhol and the Chilean Eugenio Dittborn, for example, would there be any question of a hierarchy of the central and peripheral? Connected by their use of serial silkscreened photographic imagery, and perhaps also by a certain feeling for the vulnerability of the human person, the mood of Warhol would exhibit the cynicism/indifference (not meant derogatively), and Dittborn the aspirations/miseries which Paulo Venâncio describes. And, while for Warhol 'pop' means consumer goods and mass media icons, for Dittborn pop is connected with anonymous history, collective memory and the unofficial utterance...

Pure research, testing of the limits of art, challenging perception and habit on the one side; awareness and response to the great contradictions of the immediate human and natural environment on the other: these two sides of the artist are in continuous interaction. In the most creative periods a number of projects unfold together: rejection of the Beaux-Arts model of art, and of the frameworks of museum, monument, picture; adoption and transformation of ideas from the Western metropolis; and an effort by intellectuals to move closer to the common experience, without resorting to populism, localism, or the kind of 'illustration of politics' demanded of artists by most left political parties, without sacrificing any philosophic, aesthetic, linguistic or epistemological resource. Obviously this has been a flexible borderline which has encompassed different kinds of practice, although disputes over the need for a politically functional art have often been intense.

Brazil embodies the fascinating paradox of adopting 'concrete art' in the '50s (mediated by Max Bill's visits to the country). Representing for Brazilian artists the 'absolutely modern', concretism also carried with it the orderly rationalities of Swiss-German industrialized life. It was the tensions of applying these to the Brazilian tropical and 'under-developed' environment which resulted in the intellectually and artistically powerful Neo-concrete movement of the '60s, particularly the innovatory work of Lygia Clark and Hélio Oiticica. One very characteristic product of the neo-concrete movement was Lygia Pape's (b. 1929) *Book of Creation* (1959). It recast the creation story as a series of lucid geometric metaphors, card constructions which could be manipulated by the reader, combining the 'cosmological' and the playful strains in abstraction. It expressed the enthusiasm of the Brazilians to take on and surpass the modern movement. Mauricio Cirne's photographs of the Book's pages deposited around the city of Rio, seem to re-immerse this 'pure' research in everyday popular life by a beautiful and spontaneous sleight of hand, as if testing the mental construct in the chaotically rich reality (we feel an artist's thought for which there

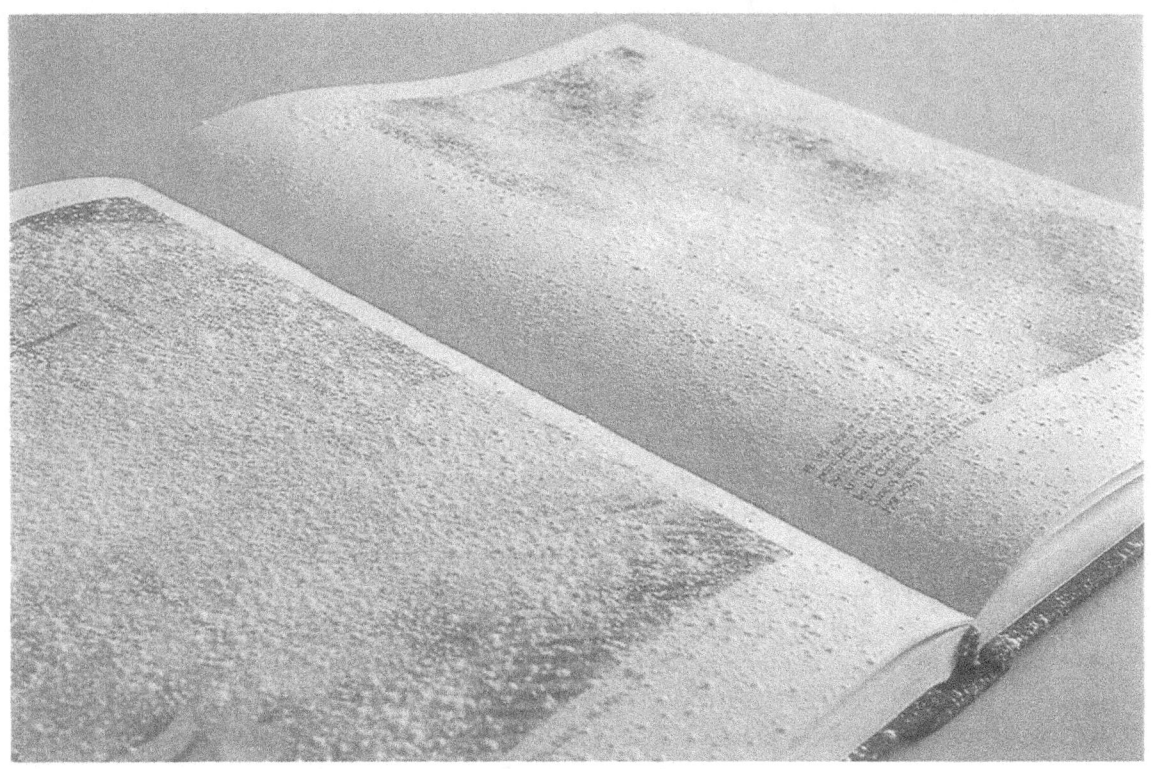

Waltercio Caldas, **Matisse with talc** 1978.

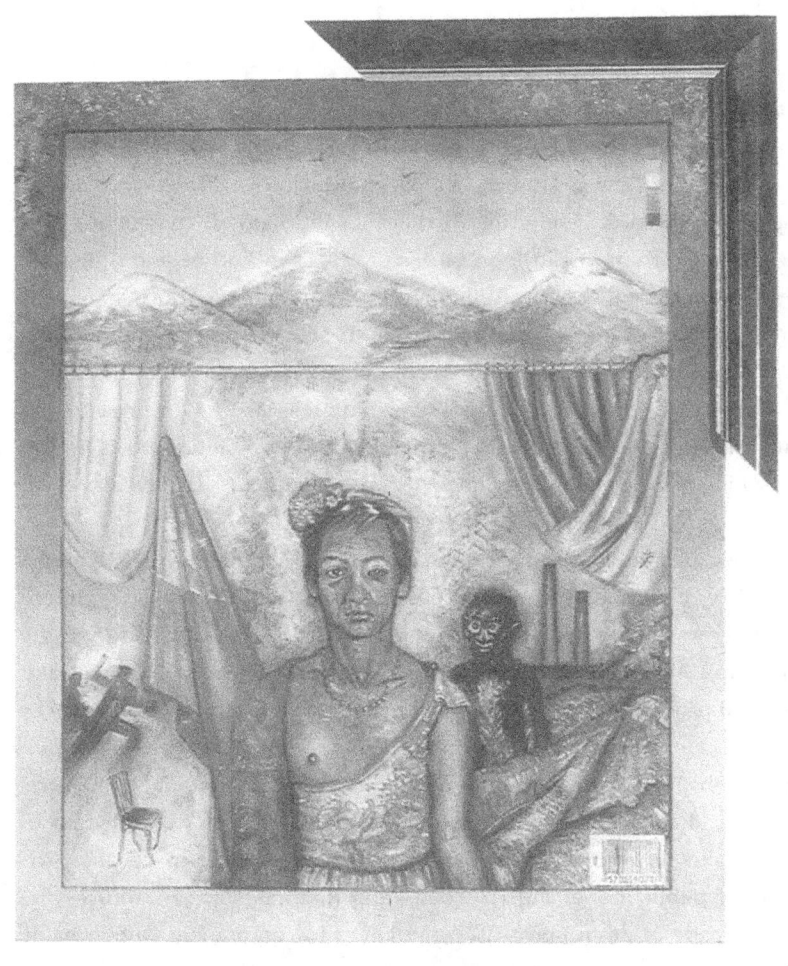

Juan Davila, **Frida** 1987
Oil on canvas, 60 × 50 cms.

was not yet an institutional frame, a museum depository).

The Noigandres group of concrete poets in Sâo Paulo, as well as Mira Schendel's drawings and her 'sculptures' made of knotted rice paper (which she called *Droguinhas*, or "scraps of nothing") introduced the notion of the 'void' to Brazilian art (paralleling Yves Klein, Piero Manzoni, Lucio Fontana and John Cage's proposals in Europe and America). Negation has been a powerful philosophical resource in the development of avant-garde strategies in Latin America, and can still be strongly felt in this book. As the optimism of the '50s and early '60s turned to the repression and fear of military rule, and use of the public space changed its implications, new tactics appeared. Cildo Meireles' work represents par excellence the interaction of pure perceptual research with the possibilities of activism in the social space, resulting in a rich body of 'politicised conceptualism' from 1968 on, which is still unknown in Europe.

Argentina had known an abstract-concrete movement even earlier than Brazil's (Fontana was active in Buenos Aires in the late '40s). By the '60s, avant-garde activity centered around the Instituto de Tella, directed by Romero Brest and later the CAYC, directed by Jorge Glusberg, both in Buenos Aires. The Duchampian ready-made, Fluxus tactics of events and happenings, kinetic and process art, were transformed in an Argentinian context, notably by Leopoldo Maler with his memorable 'typewriter on fire' (*Homage*, 1974), by Lea Lublin with her sensorial labyrinths, by Victor Grippo with his potato works and his translation of a rural earth-oven to bake bread in the city-centre (see p.87), and by Marta Minujin, first in complex sensory-symbolic environments and then in her later series of spectacular 'de-monumentalization' of public monuments by rebuilding them as popular culture (the Buenos Aires Obelisk made of raisin buns, 1979, the James Joyce Tower in Dublin made from bread, 1980, and a huge replica of the famous tango-singer Carlos Gardel on fire, 1981).

Chile was sealed off by a cultural boycott during the early years of the Pinochet dictatorship in the late '70s (partly as a result of policies modelled on attitudes towards. Franco's Spain), and Chile's 'culture of resistance' was known mainly through the activities of exile groups. But more recently we have been made aware of the much greater complexity of unofficial cultural life in Chile under authoritarian rule. A sophisticated and comprehensive analysis and response to every aspect of this rule was made by intellectuals in a way which brought into close contact social scientists, poets, artists, film-makers, photographers and others. Despite all difficulties, an avant-garde, or *Avanzada*, was intensely active in the mid '70s and early '80s, with forms of conceptual art, photo-text, installations, body-works and performance.[21]

In the traumatic conditions, these professional artists faced a burning self-question: *Que vamos a hacer?* ('What are we going to do?'). It was as if the challenge to 'art', as an institution and a set of protocols, became inseparable from an attempt by intellectuals to move closer to the experience of the mass of people - just at a moment when the military regime was trying to cement social, geographical, sexual demarcations more rigidly than ever. This is felt in Dittborn's paintings, in the performances of Carlos Leppe and others, in Lotty Rosenfeld's interventions in the street, or the body-actions of the writer-artist Diamela Eltit, whose words might sum up their attitude: "That is why I want to remain in a precarious and isolated integrity and leave open the gap with the multitudes."[22]

Irony became a weapon. As the writer D.C. Muecke once observed, irony has a kind of gyroscopic function of keeping life liveable; it can be used both to destabilise the excessively stable and established, and to stablilise the unstable, arbitrary and chaotic.[23] The Chilean body-works become very poignant in this sense, both wittily questioning the institution of art through the living body of the artist, and offering the body as a stabilizer, as "the ultimate value" (Eltit). Two examples will bear this out: Carlos Leppe's event *Artist's Proof* (1981), where two bodies became printers, transferring the inked word "Activo" from one person's skin to another's by embracing, and Eltit's performances in marginal zones (brothels, flophouses, jails in Santiago), involving forms of self-wounding, and identifying the artist's body with the pains of the social body.

◆

The 'language of the body' provides one of many links with the seminal works of Lygia Clark (1925-1988) and of Hélio Oiticica (1937-1980). The reputation of these two artists has been gradually spreading outside their immediate national context as it becomes more and more clear that their work not only goes to the heart of the major artistic issues of the '60s and '70s, conceived in non-national terms, but also does so in specific cultural ways which change the meaning of those issues. Their ideas developed separately but they had an intense on-going dialogue and shared respect for each others' work. Of this dialogue, (and

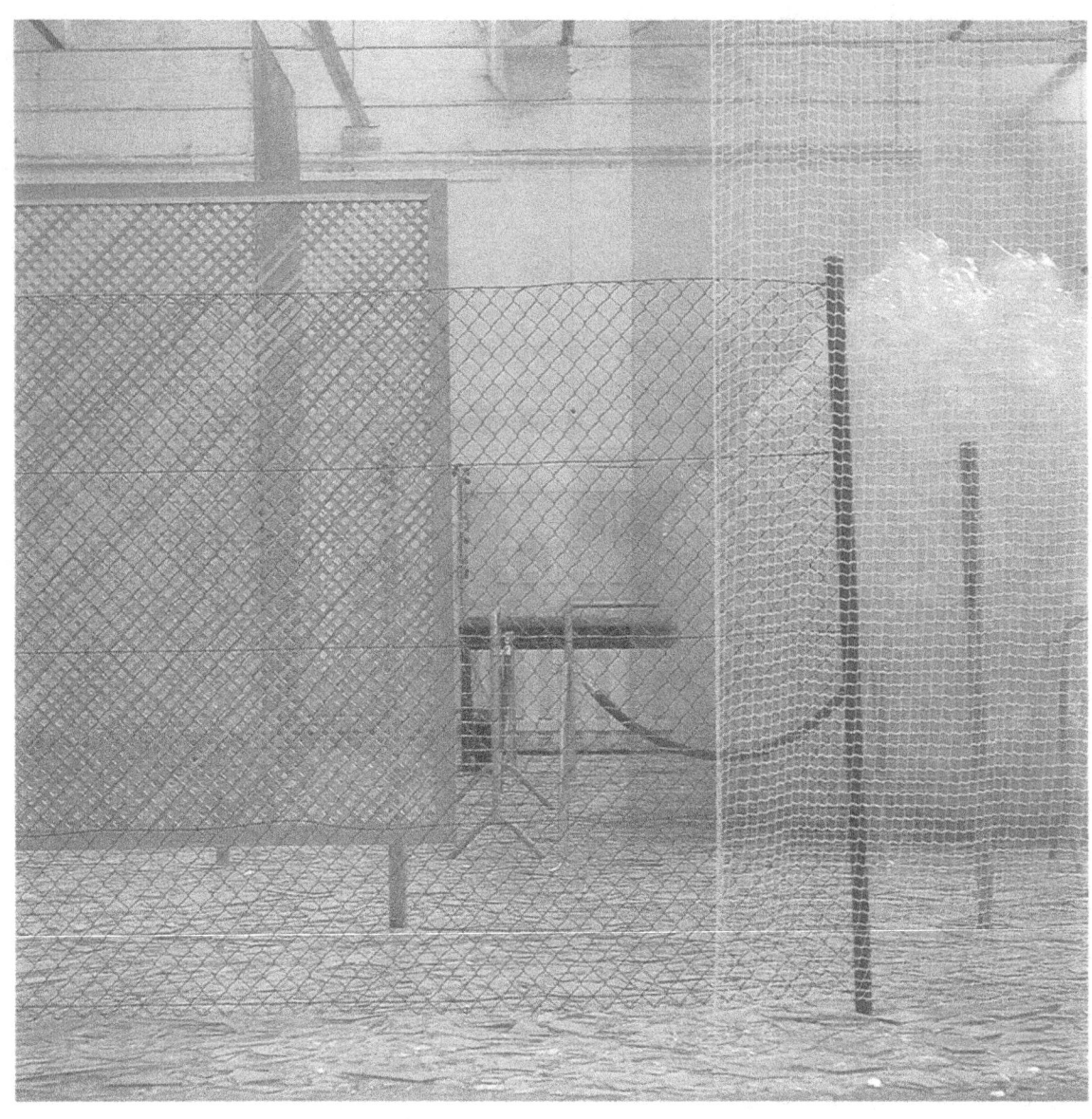

Cildo Meireles, **A Traves ('Through')** 1989. (detail).
Kanaal Art Foundation, Kortrijk, 1989.

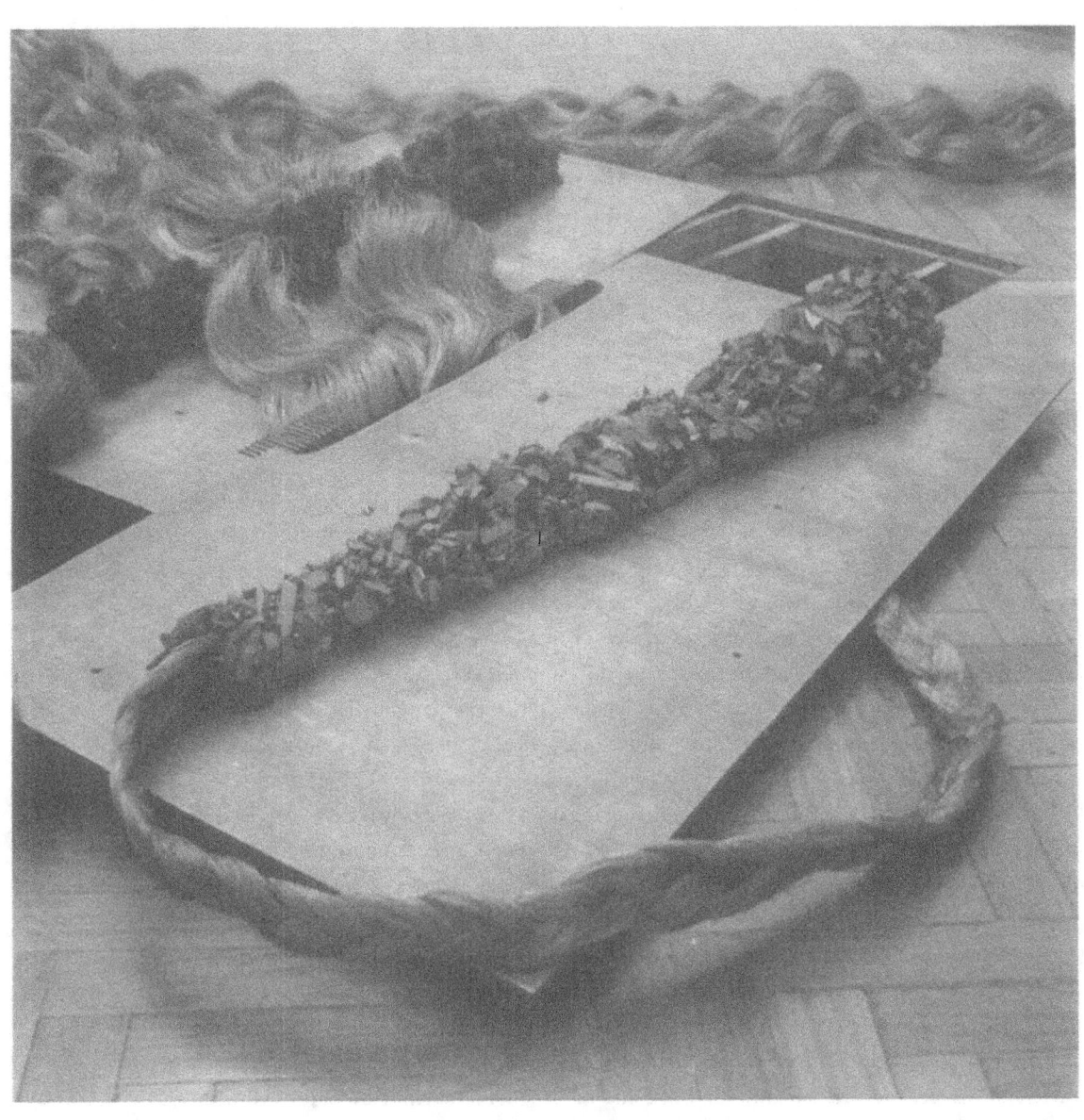

Tunga. **Lizart Nº 3** (detail) 1989.
Stedelijk Museum, Amsterdam, 1989.

of the dialogue of both artists with 'the spectator') Lygia Clark has said: "Hélio is like the outside of the glove, very much linked to the exterior world. I am the inside, and the two of us exist from the moment there is a hand which puts on the glove."[24]

Lygia Clark began in the vein of geometric abstraction, but by the early 1960s had broken with the traditional idea of the sculpture or painting as a detached object in which the body's energy and the artist's expressive power are somehow captured, frozen. She had begun to work directly with her own body and those of others. Her 'sculptures' had become simple, flexible, somewhat organic devices made of rubber bands, polythene, air, stones and so on, which were to be handled, worn, or passed from one person to another. If earlier art had aimed to produce a compressed sign of vitality 'out there', Lygia Clark's signs were inner, representing people's complex sensations of physical existence and identity "to and among themselves". So convinced did Lygia Clark become of the efficacy of her insights into the relationship between the physical and metaphorical in the body's experience, that towards the end of her life she actually used her devices in a therapeutic treatment for people with mental disturbances. These devices would revive memories of the body's earliest experiences.

At each stage of her work, Lygia Clark pushed her concept to the point of precipitating a crisis of meaning, which revealed the limits of the structure for getting closer to the "complex and dynamic creativity of life", and so laid the basis for the next stage. In the process, traditional certainties, boundaries, identities, were thrown into question: between male and female, between self and other, self and nature, between child and adult, between what can be spoken and what can't. She went into a completely new area where 'art' was both efficacious cure and philosophical speculation.

Hélio Oiticica, who died in 1980 at the age of 43, positioned himself audaciously between the avant-garde, Brazilian popular culture, the realities of 'under-development' and '60s radicalism. Like Lygia Clark, he began with a Mondrian-like formal analysis of the pictorial order: the plane, figure/ground relationships, the frame. His early experiments were to move from that plane to the environmental space, and from a purely optical to a 'bodily' sensation of colour. His formal models became the *Bolide* ('Fireball' or 'Flaming Meteor' in Portuguese), the *Penetrable* and the *Parangolé*, each of them objects conceived as 'energy centres' which draw spectators close ("like a fire", as he once remarked) and invite manipulation. From then on, his acute analysis of the new art movements in Europe and

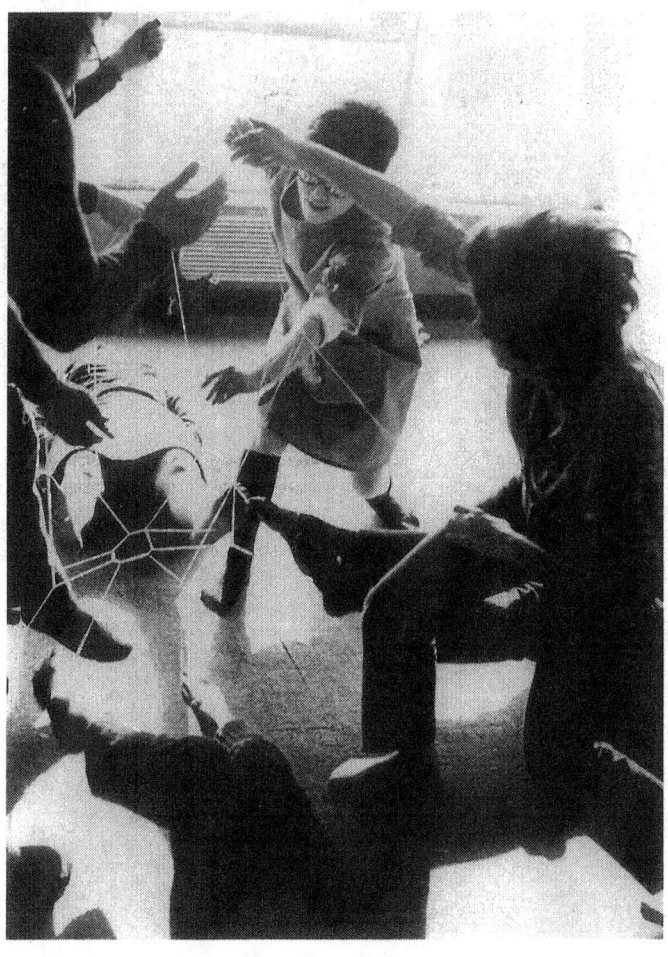

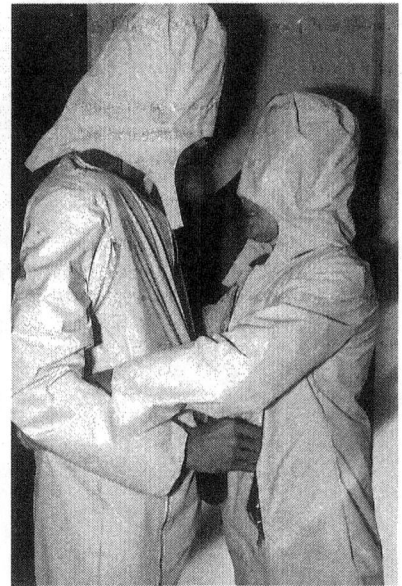

Lygia Clark, **Collective Body - Mandala**, elastic web,
Rio de Janeiro 1969.

Lygia Clark, **The I and the You (clothing-body-clothing)**, touch dialogue with exchanged male
and female attributes linked by rubber umbilical,
Rio de Janeiro 1969.

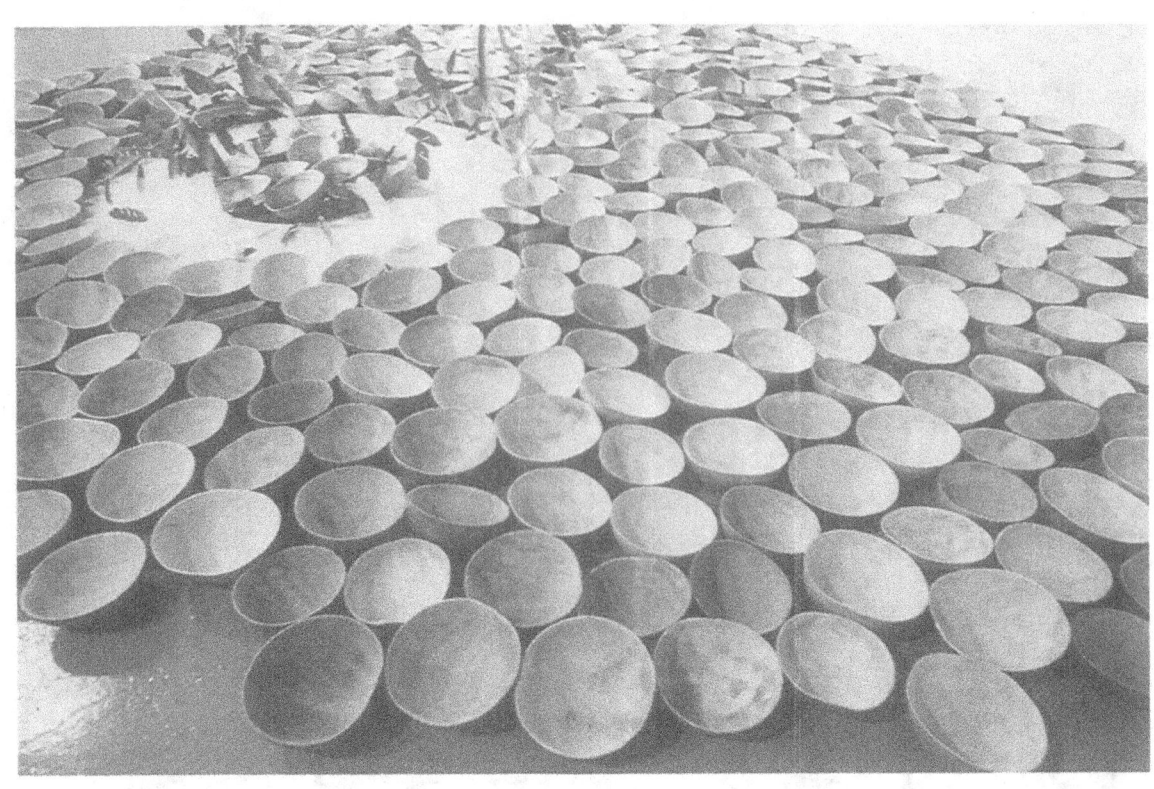

Roberto Evangelista/Regina Vater, **Nika Uiicana** 1989.
Dedicated to Chico Mendes. 300 Amazonian gourds and several hundred bird feathers.
Installed at the Clocktower Gallery, New York.

and North America became closely bound up with his self-exposure to Brazil's popular culture, and to the powerful contradictions in the social reality of Rio de Janeiro. Crossing class barriers and living for periods in Mangueira (one of Rio's *favelas*, or shanty-towns) resulted in new work concepts. Among these, *Parangolé* is perhaps the most daring.

Although *Parangolé* took the physical form of 'capes', and sometimes banners and 'standards', the word stood for a mode of creative-expressive behaviour rather than objects as such. The Brazilian critic Frederico Morais called it "a programme, a vision of the world, an ethic".[25] Here, in a hybrid, he brought together his refined assimilation of European constructivism, his advanced notions of spectator-participation (that creation is a dialogue and the object has no status outside its 'relational' role), Brazil's popular culture of the body, his own sexuality, and the exaltations and sufferings of the mass of people as he had intuited them. The *Capes* (incorporating cloth, plastic, earth, words and so on) are internal-external, and individual-collective, dialogues. Wearing them, running or dancing in them, reveals things to the wearer, at the same time as it projects messages to those around, as a kind of 'clothing-utterance'.

The critic Carlos Zilio has discussed Oiticica's work also in terms of a "concept of crisis". Inclined always towards "the precarious, the unstable", Oiticica conducted a "permanent deconstruction and disarticulation of the categories instituted by art, without looking for a resolution or synthesis."[26] Both Lygia Clark and Hélio Oiticica were extraordinarily restless people, and both knew the price they paid for abandoning the artisanal side of art. A key value for them was *vivencias*, or "lived thought". Clark interpreted this mind-body unity in terms of the 'interior' life of psychological experience, Oiticica in terms of the 'exterior' life of behaviour, culture, sociability, work/leisure (hence Lygia Clark's glove-metaphor), but neither saw any hard and fast boundary between them.

FOOTNOTES

1. Information, (ed. Kynaston McShine), New York: Museum of Modern Art, 1970, p. 103.

2. José Jaoquin Brunner, 'Esta Fragil Materia Suspendida', in *Chile Vive. Memoria Activa*, Santiago de Chile: SENECA, 1987, p. 10.

3. See Jimmie Durham, 'Here at the Centre of the World', *Third Text* No 5 (Winter 1988/9), p. 21.

4. Jean-Hubert Martin, interviewed in *Art Press*, Paris, May 1989.

5. Dorine Mignot, "Turn the Map Upside Down", U-ABC, Amsterdam: Stedelijk Museum, 1989, p. 17.

6. Coco Fusco, 'The Border Art Workshop/Taller de Arte Fronterizo: Interview with Guillermo Gómez-Peña and Emily Hicks', *Third Text*, No 7 (Summer 1989), p.64-65.

7. Ibid., p. 76.

8. If present trends continue, it is estimated that 85% of the Brazilian population will live in the cities by the year 2000.

9. Ronald Kay, *Del Espacio de Aca*, Santiago de Chile: Editores Asociados, 1980.

10. For example, Amazonia contains one in five of all known bird species and at least 2000 species of fish (Ten times as many as in the whole of Europe). See *Fight for the Forest: Chico Mendes in his Own Words*, London: Latin American Bureau, 1989, p. 44.

11. Darrell A. Posey, 'Alternatives to Forest Destruction: Lessons from the Mêbêngôkre Indians', *The Ecologist*, Nov/Dec 1989, p. 244.

12. J.J. Brunner, 'Cultura y Sociedad en Chile', *Chile Vive*, Circulo de Bellas Artes, Madrid, 1987, p. 20.

13. Coco Fusco, op. cit., p. 68.

14. Oswald de Andrade, *Pau-Brasil Poetry*, 1924. Both manifestos are reprinted in English translation in Dawn Ades, *Art in Latin America: The Modern Era*, London: The South Bank Centre/Yale University Press, 1989.

15. Adriana Valdes, 'From Another Periphery: 17 Mail Paintings', *Eugenio Dittborn*, George Paton Gallery, Melbourne, Australia, 1985, p. 6.

16. Tensions between centre and periphery have always been part of the history of 20th century art, more so than is usually acknowledged. Cf, Kazimir Malevich's remark about his origins in the Russian hinterland: "Reality was all around me, but the means of depicting it were in Moscow where famous artists lived"; and the journeys of many early modernists from rural, sometimes feudal, birthplaces to the metropolis (Brancusi, Moholy-Nagy, Buñuel, and others).

17. See Paulo Venâncio Filho, "Situaçôes Limites", *Cildo Meireles, Tunga*, Kortrijk, Kanaal Art Foundation, 1989.

18. "Thus the art practices in fashion ten years ago, such as body art, land art or performance art...are very close to our reality today, irrespective of the international standards, precisely because they echo the drama of our everyday life...The use of the body as a support for art is very familiar to us, but this familiarity is gained at the cost of other sorts of deprivation. Recent developments in art do not define our scene, but rather our exposure to poverty and pain, to the loneliness of individual lives". "Una Ponencia del CADA", *Ruptura* , 1982. Quoted by Nelly Richard in 'Margins and Institutions' (see following note).

19. Nelly Richard, 'Margins and Institutions: Art in Chile since 1973'. *Art & Text* No 21, May/June 1986 (special issue).

20. Paulo Venâncio Filho, op. cit.

21. See Nelly Richard, op. cit.

22. Diamela Eltit, *Vagamente Famosos* 'Vaguely Famous', slide sequence included in *Margins and Institutions: Art in Chile 1973-1989*, The Showroom, London, 1989.

23. D.C. Muecke, *Irony and the Ironic*, London: Methuen, 1982.

24. Lygia Clark, quoted in *Veja* magazine, Rio de Janeiro, December 1986.

25. Frederico Morais, *Pequeno Roteiro Cronologico das Invençôes de Hélio Oiticica*, Rio de Janeiro, 1980, p. 2.

26. Letter to the writer, May 1989.

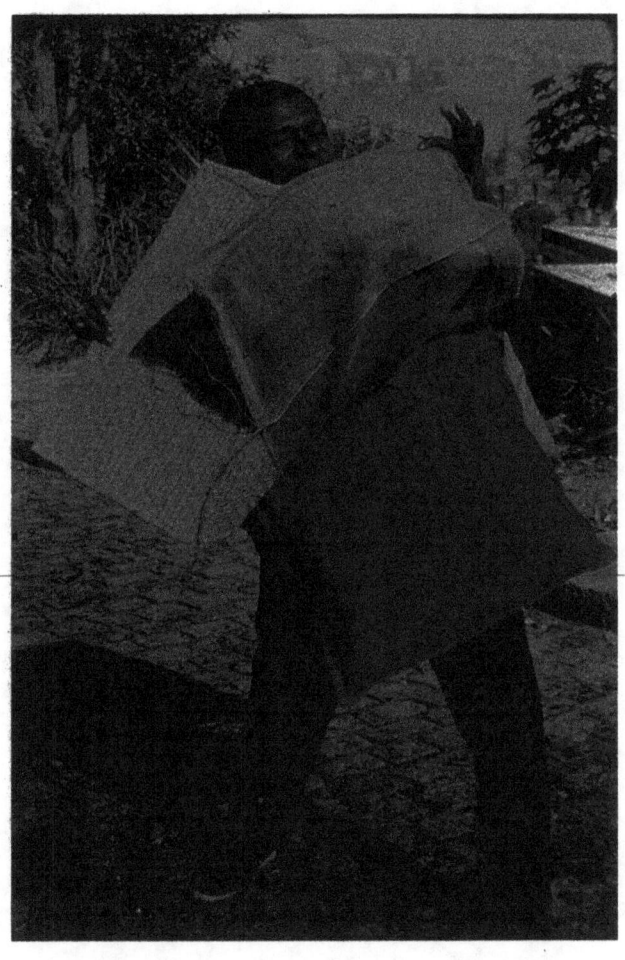

Hélio Oiticica, **Parangolé - Cape II** "Encorporo la Revolta" ("I Embody Revolt") 1967.
Projeto HO, Rio de Janeiro.

Material Poetics

The moment seems to demand art capable of a multiplicity of meanings. Art which, in relation to a notion such as the 'Latin American', would discourage simplistic and hackneyed responses. Works which would bring forward new and complex metaphors (in the original Greek meaning of the term, 'to carry over': "the transference of aspects of one object to another object, so that the second object is spoken of as if it were the first")[1], rich not only in themselves, but in the sparks they would set off by contact and comparison with those of the other artists. Meanings would arise from the material, its specific nature and its location in space, from art's traditional attachment to the sensory and physical. These were some of the starting points for the exhibition and this book.

The words multiplicity and metaphor are not meant to suggest something vague. This book could also be seen in terms of a number of strategies for "approaching closer to reality", a process which for each artist is intimately connected to a polemical examination, or riposte, or refusal, of art as an institution. Again, these strategies are diverse and individual in all their particular details. The differences between them are as striking as any similarity: for example the contrast between a 'harmonic' approach such as you find in Regina Vater's and Roberto Evangelista's *Nika Uiícana* (a particular way of referring to ecological and cultural problems), and a discordant aesthetic of violent clashes, as in Juan Davila's painting.

Another premise for this book was that the works would signal across continental borders and across national borders within the continent (even though the artists might not know one another or be aware of one another's work). This is symbolised by the combinations of localised and non-localised materials and references mentioned in the preface. Every reader will see different kinds of signal. One, which connects several artists, is the presence of metaphors which imply 'potential' and 'restriction': Victor Grippo's *Analogies*, in which potatoes and beans, basic foodstuffs of the continent, apparently prosaic and humble, demonstrate their latent energies; Cildo Meireles' *Southern Cross* and his *Sermon on the Mount: Fiat Lux*, which both obliquely suggest the eruptions of a fire which is kept repressed; or Jac Leirner's *The Hundreds* - money as official inertia and as the unexpected medium of a whole mass of popular voicings. (Having taken out such specific meanings, they should probably be put back again, among the possible other ones).

One particularly fascinating link-up between the works is the thematic of the body. Lygia Clark's and Hélio Oiticica's great theme had been the body, and, as the Brazilian critic

Paulo Sérgio Duarte has pointed out, they experimented with abolishing the artist's role of mediator, since there is no body 'represented' between artist and spectator.[2] By contrast, the works here present an extraordinary complexity of mediation. The body can be inferred in a remarkable number of ways which go beyond the traditional methods of direct depiction.

In Tunga's work, the body is constantly inferred by references which change drastically in scale (for example, from molar to mountain), and weave in and out between named entities (hair, comb, brain) and orderly or chaotic force-fields (magnetized fragments, plaited or loose wire) in such a way as to immerse the human body in myriads of other physical and notional bodies. Many of Cildo Meireles' works, notably his participatory environment, *Blindhotland*, play the visual sense against the evidence of the other senses to produce a new elasticity in our relationship to space. In Waltercio Caldas' work the body is inferred by almost vertiginous gaps, or gulfs, between what you see and what you think: the mind is addressed in its symbiosis with the body, and vice versa. Jac Leirner has made a series of sculptures in which the standardized and mechanically-produced components of cigarette-packs become metaphors for the lung, (as well as an exploration of sculptural morphology). In Eugenio Dittborn's Airmail Paintings you feel an almost limitless interrelationship between graphic marks and traces and human flesh and blood. Victor Grippo's *Analogy* is grounded in the very incongruity of the proposal that the potato can stand for human consciousness. For Roberto Evangelista, the Indian gourds used in *Nika Uiícana* have a relationship with the crown of the head. Juan Davila does, of course, 'depict', but confounds any notion of *the* body. In his paintings, 'body' is one of the main matrices (along with 'landscape' and 'interior') for shattering traditional unities, and for amalgamating things which are not supposed to touch. It is plain to see that 'body' is both carnal and sexual, and an argument of visual codes.

But again, comparisons between the artists could be made in a completely different register, a more abstract or philosophical one. One can often see, for example, a dialectic taking place between 'presence' and 'absence', between image and erasure of image, or void, between thing and shadow or "ghost version" (Jac Leirner). This seems to me a vital aspect of the artist's investigation, or testing, of reality, the always-ambiguous relationship between the real and fictive, which is here pursued into all kinds of areas: the social, the political, the philosophical, the scientific, the sexual. The topical, contingent, agitated image as against the blank, silent, null-and-void. The Indian critic Geeta Kapur has referred to the concept of the void in classical Indian metaphysics as "the inexhaustible potential". In one of her writings, she has memorably described its use in the Ajanta murals, in a way which I believe allows us to make another 'transcontinental' connection:

> The figures advance from depths which are never defined, pressing forward, one after another, maintaining a poise between the exuberance of life and the stillness of the depths....Everything is simultaneously present, approaching the surface and held together in a compact spatial structure, through multiple, interacting viewpoints and perspectives.[3]

FOOTNOTES

1. Terence Hawkes, *Metaphor*, London: Methuen 1972 p.1.

2. Paulo Sérgio Duarte, interview in *Lygia Clark e Hélio Oiticica* (ed. Luciano Figueiredo and Glória Ferreira), Rio de Janeiro: Funarte 1986, p. 76.

3. Geeta Kapur, *Pictorial Space: a Point of View on Contemporary Indian Art*, (exhibition catalogue), Lalit Kala Akademi, New Delhi, 1978.

How to Build Troubled Skies

Although made up of symbols already loaded with meaning (which refer to the circumstances of the work's commission)[1] How To Build Cathedrals possesses a formal syntax which resists intensely the kind of reductionist reading usually implied by the 'symbolic'. Perhaps this is the reason for its singularity and integrity. A strange ambiguity arises from its play between redundancy and information, the sharply defined and the diffuse.

Money - the foundation of How To Build Cathedrals - first appeared in Cildo's work in 1969. If, as an artist, he sets himself against repetitive 'style' (which he likes to call "mental craftsmanship"), the problem of Value - with money as its most objective symbol - has always been one of his key reference points.

The Tree of Money (1969) was simply a stack of 100 one-cruzeiro bills bound with elastic bands (as is done in banks) and placed on a pedestal. A label said the price of the work was 2000 cruzeiros, a jump of 20 times the real, or use, value. Here the relationship of the art object with the market was stripped naked through the metalinguistic figure of money buying itself.

In How To Build Cathedrals, the circulation of value denoted by the coins is taken up by the central column of communion wafers, which prolongs and elevates their roundness, as if the wafers were themselves coins. But to Roman Catholics the wafer is a symbol whose value lies in its being, physically, the body of Christ (God made flesh).

Paradoxically, it is precisely there, in the delicate, rarified column of wafers, where the work almost dematerialises itself (by contrast with the hardness and physicality of coins and bones), that an invisible inflation of the body occurs.

The bones - metonym for the body - building a suspended cemetery where our eyes expect to find the 'sky', suggest an extermination: the continuous extermination of the producers by the predators, according to Cildo.

And after recognizing this devaluation of the body, our gaze is induced to descend again the column of wafers which functions as a kind of central cortex, and return to the coins.

A possible (e)sc(h)atology insinuates itself. The golden brightness, the 'sacred' solemnity of How To Build Cathedrals becomes strangely intensified when we remember that value is nourished from gold and excrement - two psychological attributes of money - from everything and nothing, from the hungry horizon of homo economicus, this "finite being", as Foucault calls him, "who passes, spends and wastes his life preoccupied with escaping the imminence of death"[2].

Lu Menezes, Rio de Janeiro, 1990.

1. How To Build Cathedrals was the result of a commission by the Brazilian firm Iochpe (represented by Evelyn Berg and the critic Frederico Morais), for the exhibition Missions - 300 years. This exhibition was concerned with the historical episode of the Jesuit Missions in southern Brazil: 'theoretic estates' based on the domination of the Indian population and cattle raising, which removed the Indians from the land and led to their extermination.
2. Michel Foucault, The Order of Things, Tavistock Publications, 1970.

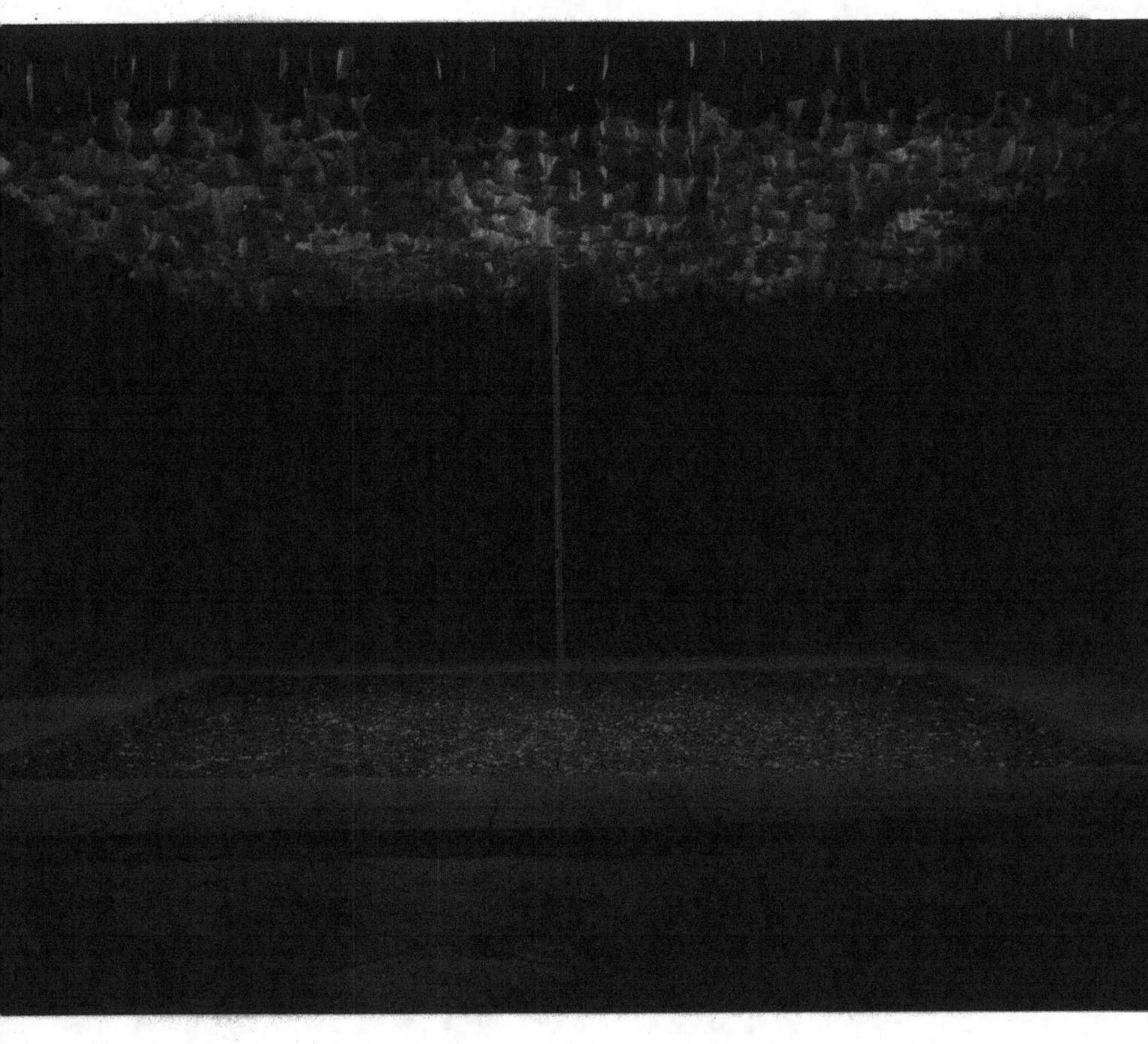

Massão/Missões (How to Build Cathedrals) 1987.
600,000 metal coins, 2000 bones, 800 communion wafers, 86 paving stones, black cloth.

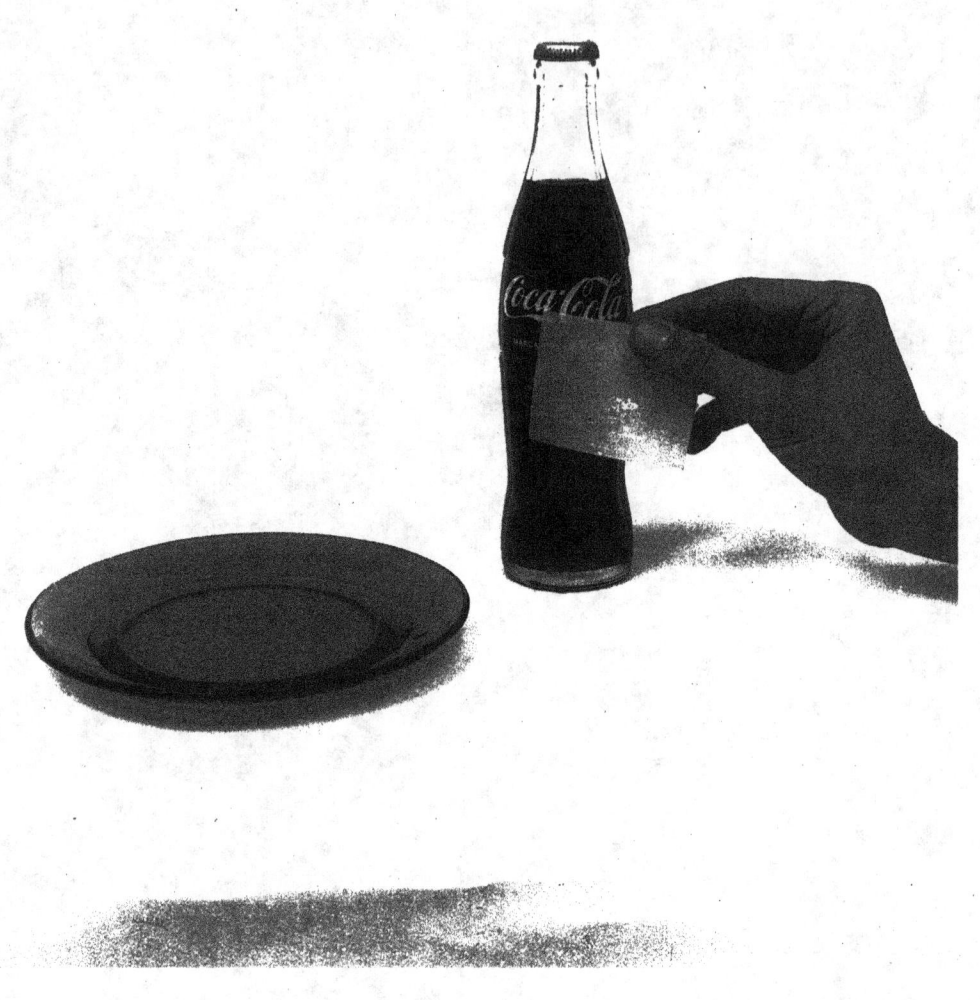

Insertion into Ideological Circuits: Coca-Cola project 1970.
Information and/or political opinions printed on Coca-Cola bottles, which circulate on a deposit system in Brazil.

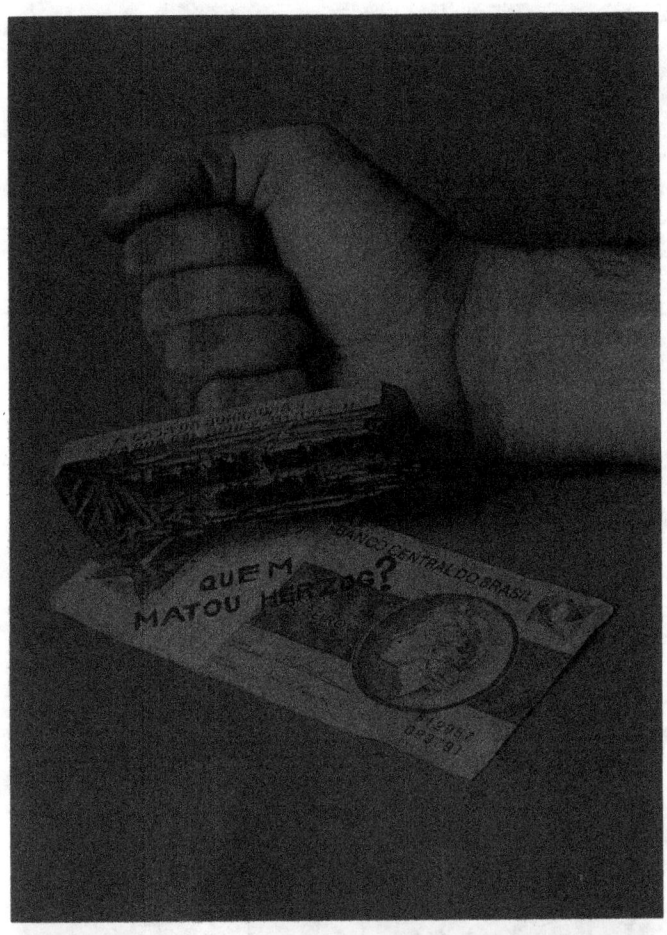

Insertion into Ideological Circuits: Banknote project 1970-75. Who Killed Herzog?
In 1975 Vladimir Herzog, a well-known socialist journalist was arrested by the CODI ('Information Service' of the Brazilian army) and died two days later in custody. The authorities claimed he committed suicide, and it was public disbelief of this claim which marked the beginning of effective opposition to military government.

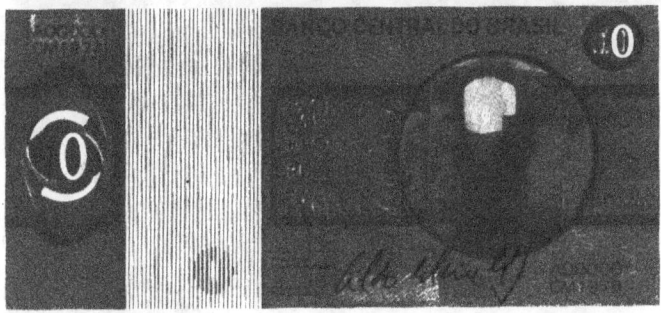

Zero cruzeiro bill 1978. Print on paper.

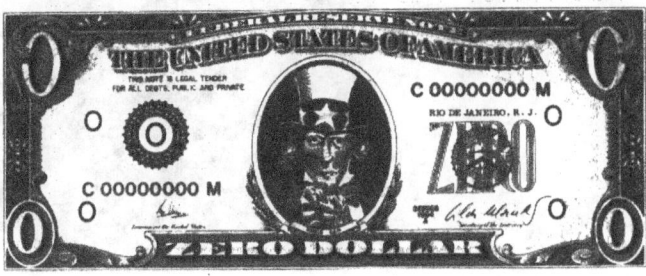

Zero dollar bill 1984. Print on paper.

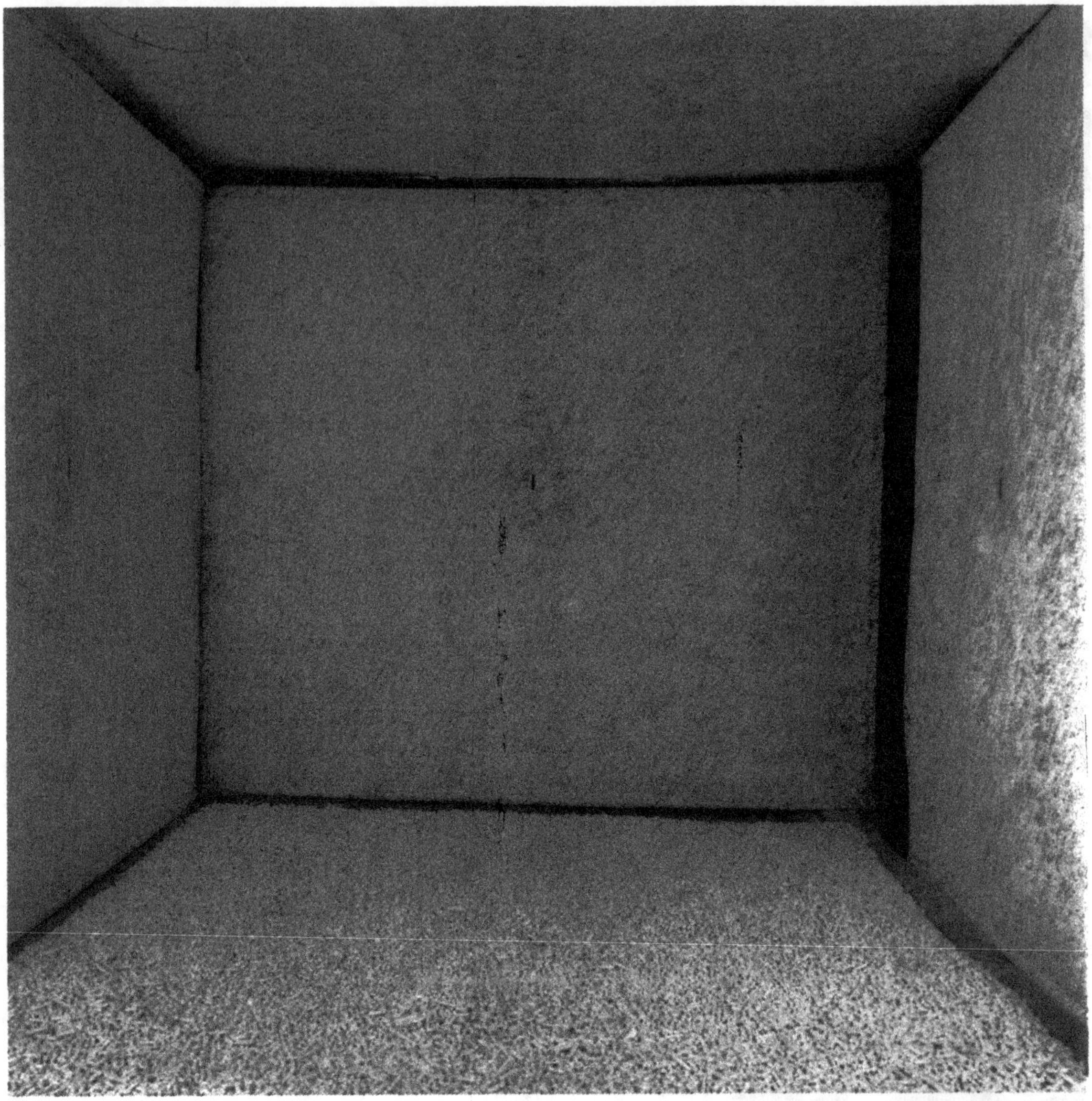

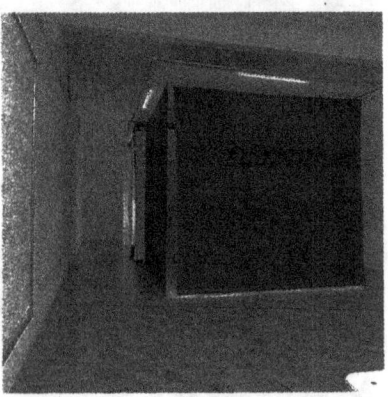

Cinza (Grey, Ash) 1984/86.
Two cubical rooms, each approx 330 × 330 cms, one lined with canvases whitened with school chalk, the other with canvases charcoaled black. Chalk and charcoal on the floor.

The piece which Cildo Meireles chose to place at the front of a book about his work published by Funarte in Brazil, was a box made in 1970. A small bronze plaque on the lid carries the words: "TO BE CURVED WITH THE EYES". Open the box to find two iron bars, one straight, the other curved, mounted inside, and above them in the lid a red enamel plaque which says: "TWO BARS OF EQUAL LENGTH AND CURVED". Meireles intends this box to be on show at all his exhibitions. Noting the passage of time, the spectators would almost involuntarily see the box as "proving and/or contesting that the act of looking, the gaze, is a 'physical force'...."[4] Even if we immediately take the whole thing as a conceit, we realize that what Meireles is placing at issue here is seeing, looking, as a determinant in the real world.

At the end of the 1960s and in the early 1970s, Meireles' meditations on space, visuality, and on dimension were poetically and paradoxically encapsulated in boxes and similar devices. After conducting a *reductio ad absurdum* of classical Euclidian and perspectival space by constructing a sort of portable indoor corner, a blind trap of the bourgeois' 'own four walls', which was shown in various places, including the beach on one occasion, Meireles moved to investigate space in its multiple connotations: as "physical, geometric, historical, psychological, topological and anthropological". One box in his *Arte Fisica* series (1969) contained a map and a bundle of 30 km of string which had been stretched along a section of the coast in the state of Rio de Janeiro.

Another box, this time a leather case in his series *Geographical Mutations* (1969), recorded an action he undertook at the frontier between the states of Rio de Janeiro and São Paulo. The nature of frontiers as mental constructs was indicated by digging a hole on either side and transferring earth, plants, etc from one hole to the other. The leather case was made as a portable version of the event. In a beautiful extension of this play on dimensions, Meireles made two exquisite finger-rings in 1970. One, pyramidical in form and made of gold had a single grain of sand inside visible through a tiny sapphire 'window' (*Desert*); the other was a version of the *Geographical Mutations: Rio - S. Paulo Frontier* in silver, sapphire, onyx and amethyst.

Southern Cross (1969-70) was a tiny cube 9 mm square. One half was made of pine, the other of oak. These trees represent mythical entities in Tupi cosmology (Tupi is one of the principle Amazonian Indian languages) and their correlation (physically rubbing their wood together) produces fire. The little cube was to be exhibited all alone in an area of "at least 200 square metres". Even in verbal description, it acts as a superb metaphor of the Latin American space, the precariousness of the Indian presence within that space, as well as the potential power of their Fire.

No longer to have bodies, walls, limits, economic properties, physical properties, organic properties, properties. The work is against solids, a physics of solids, a politics of solids. Against all that restrains energy,

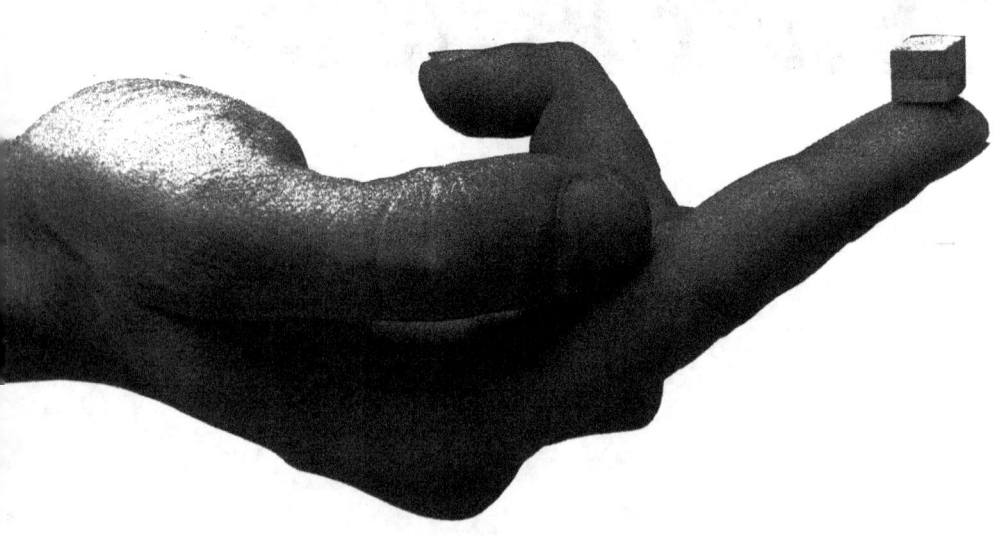

Southern Cross 1969/70.
9mm cube, pine/oak.

communication, the flux of transforming densities.[5]

Ronaldo Brito's words, in his eloquent text on Meireles, describe the artist's constant preoccupations, which are in many ways synthesised in the sensorial-philosophical environment *Blindhotland* (1975). The antique scales at the centre of *Blindhotland* arbitrate between appearance and reality. The visual sense flounders on the evidence that the balls, which all look exactly the same, are vastly different in weight, as they are in the sounds they make when rolled or thrown into the space. But with this floundering comes the sense of elasticity and expansion both in the body and in the space around us.

These perceptions of space clearly inform Meireles' more overtly political work which he began around 1970. Here must be recognized, not only the artist's personal courage in producing this work at the height of Brazil's military dictatorship (1970 was perhaps the most terrible year of the 20-year regime), but also his artistic audacity. A glance today at the catalogue of one of the earliest international surveys of 'conceptual' art, *When Attitudes Become Form*, which toured Europe in 1969-70, reveals that the artists included were still mainly occupied with formal, process and perceptual questions (no Latin Americans were invited). I say 'still' since many of the artists later produced politicized work. Cildo Meireles however, and other Latin Americans, perhaps under the pressure of events, had made the transition from an abstract to a social understanding of space as a 'flux of transforming densities'. The art work itself began to be valued less as a discreet object and more as an act of communication, an imaginative insertion into ideological and social circuits already existing. Thus Meireles made anti-imperialist texts to silk-screen on Coca-Cola bottles (which circulate on a deposit system in Brazil),1970, or messages of protest rubber-stamped on banknotes (1970-75) ("Insertions into Ideological Circuits: 1, Coca-Cola project, 2, Banknote project"). This latter, incidentally, anticipated an idea used as a tactic of resistance on a mass-scale in Chile a few years later after the Pinochet coup. A complex of ideas about the identity of the artist vis-à-vis the mass of people, and the social value of his or her work, are implicated in the formal means used. To quote Brito again, the aim was to:

....speak in the language of Insertion rather than the language of Style, to move with the flux against the fetish of the Object, to listen to the Anonymous Murmurings, rather than the Voice of the Author.[6]

In an interesting reversal, a work of 1973, instead of flowing out to objects in mass circulation, took them out of circulation and gathered them in one place. *The Sermon on the Mount: Fiat Lux* assembled a cubic mass of 126,000 boxes of matches in the centre of a room. Mirrors lined the walls, each printed with one of the celebrated beattitudes. But this storehouse of potential fire, potential light, was ringed by five 'heavies', besuited, moustachioed, hands on hips or crossed over crutch (actors in reality). The work was finally shown publicly in 1979, after being cancelled or withdrawn on three previous occasions.

The fact that the passage of time, political changes and fashion have tried to institutionalize such work, or made fun of its hopes of intervention in the real world, does not make the issues it raised, of contextualisation and efficacy, any less pressing. One of its legacies must precisely be imagination and flexibility in the use of different 'place/times'. Cildo Meireles' more recent work can partly be seen as a response to a situation in which an undeniable energy has passed to the revival of painting and a regression to all the traditional institutions of art. One of these works is *Cinza*, 1986.

Cinza, meaning both 'ash' and 'grey' in Portuguese, consists of two cabins each three by three metres, and three and a half metres high, which the spectator enters. One enclosure is lined with white canvases which have been charcoaled black, with a large quantity of loose charcoal strewn on the floor, the other is lined with black canvases which have been chalked white, with white chalk underfoot. In the centre of the charcoaled canvases, an area has been masked to leave a white image of a piece of charcoal, and vice versa for the other cabin. The tramping of people from one space to the other tends to crush the chalk and charcoal and mix the black and white to an indeterminate grey. In a cunning ambiguity, the work seems to present us with a scene of the 'ashes' of painting which is nevertheless very beautiful visually: in fact it is through the pleasures of visual ambiguity that the work brings us to think about the relation of opposites. The presence of the chalk - signifying, according to Meireles, the schoolroom, erudition - and of the charcoal, signifying the scrawled utterance in the street, bring to mind again, even in this purist ambience, the artist's two 'sources'.

Cinza doesn't provide a resolution because the question itself is unresolved. Rather than a linear development, Cildo Meireles' work can be seen in one sense as a continual meditation, modified by changing events, on the relationship of 'fine art' to 'popular culture' (or of the intellectual to the mass of people) - popular culture being understood not as the mass consumer culture of the Pop artists, but as resistance, as the struggle for a voice ∎

4. See *Cildo Meireles*, Rio de Janeiro: Funarte, 1981.

5. Ronaldo Brito, forward to *Cildo Meireles*, op. cit.

6. Ronaldo Brito, op. cit.

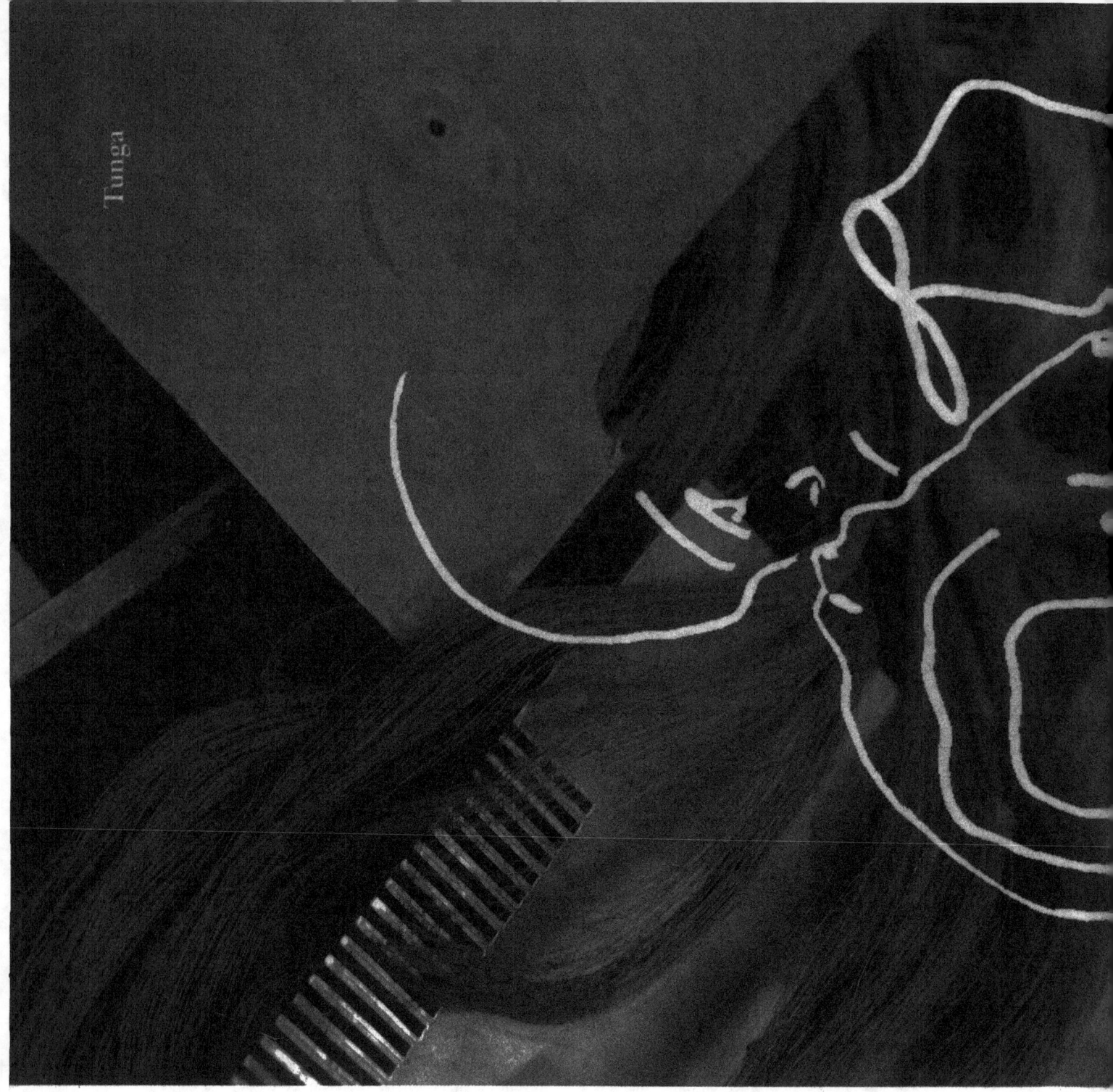

Tunga

Lizart 3 1989.
Stedelijk Museum, Amsterdam, 1989.

URINATING INVOLUNTARILY. ONCE AGAIN, WALKING. THE PRESENT NARRATIVE BEGINS WITH RE-ENCOUNTERING THE ALBINO. ONCE AGAIN

NUMBER OF ORIGINAL DRAWINGS, NOTES, AND ABOVE ALL HIS EMPATHY WITH THAT PRODIGIOUS SPIRIT.   LITTLE IS KNOWN OF KURT'S CHILDHOOD

FRAGMENTS, SKETCHES, OF HIS VISIONS (STRAIGHTFOWARD TRANSCRIPTIONS OF HIS SESSIONS WITH SCHILDER)   INDICATIONS OF HANGING. THE

AMPHIBIANS, HUGE SPECIMENS. MICHAELANGELO WAS THE FIGURE. THE IMAGE WHICH EMERGED, ASPHYXIATION. TO ASPHYXIATE MERMAIDS

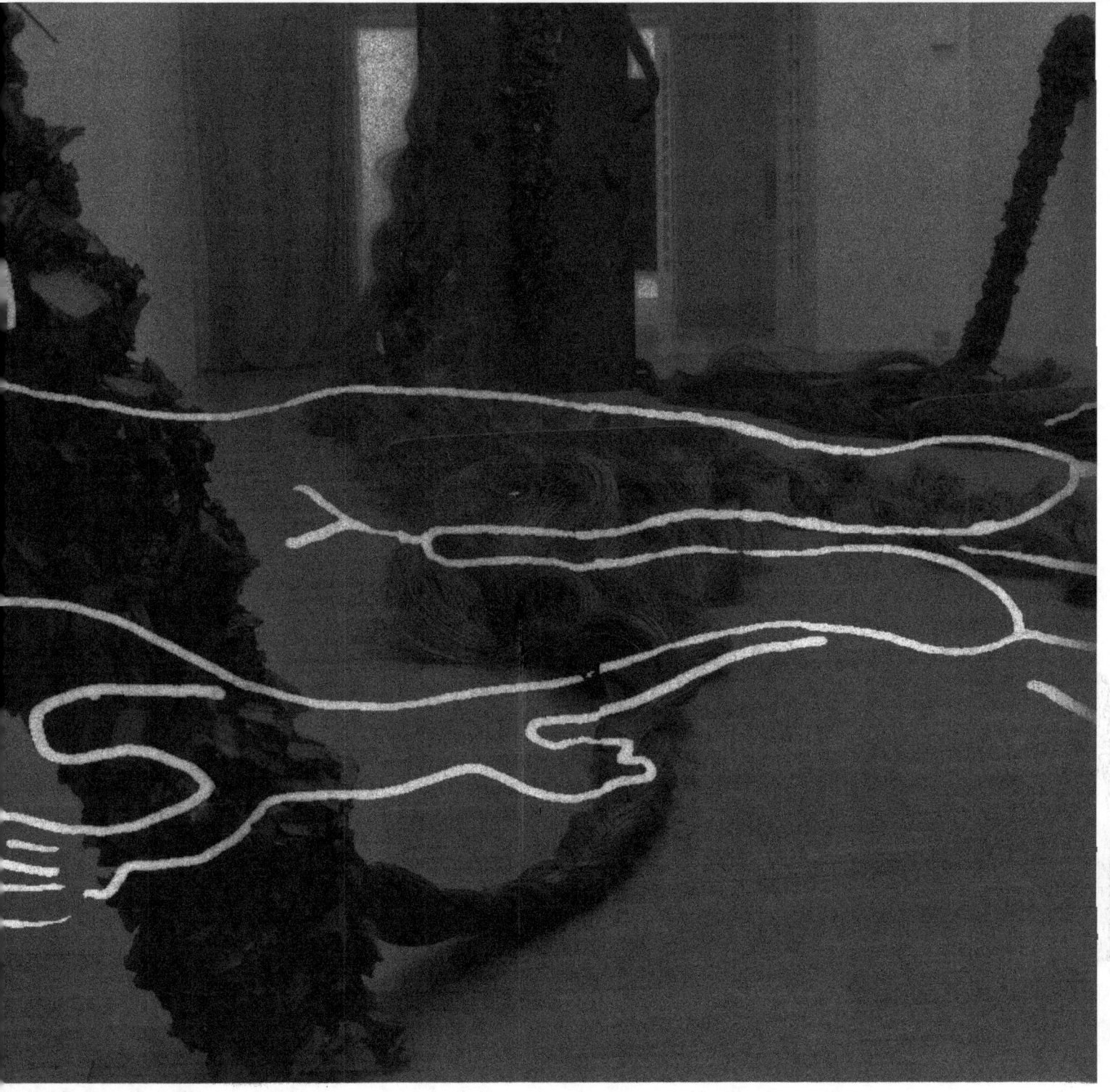

Lizart I 1989.
Whitechapel Gallery, London, 1989.

ATTERSEA PARK, MY GURU. WE WENT ONCE MORE TO LOOK AT THE ALBINO MARSUPIAL. PAUL HAD BECOME THE TEACHER. THE SECT HAD SOME
HEN HE WAS EIGHT HE HAD TO SUBMIT, ON THE PRETEXT OF A CURE, TO STROBOSCOPIC THERAPY. EPILEPSY... ONE MUST CONCLUDE THAT THIS
ONGUE, THE ERECT PENIS, "EJACULATION". STRANGULATION KEPT RECURRING IN HIS MIND. BIT BY BIT HE IDENTIFIED FIGURES, DONATELLO IN
ERMAIDS METAMORPHOSED INTO SALAMANDERS. HE CONFUSED THE SALAMANDER WITH AMIANTHUS. DOWSING THE FIRE WAS A KIND OF

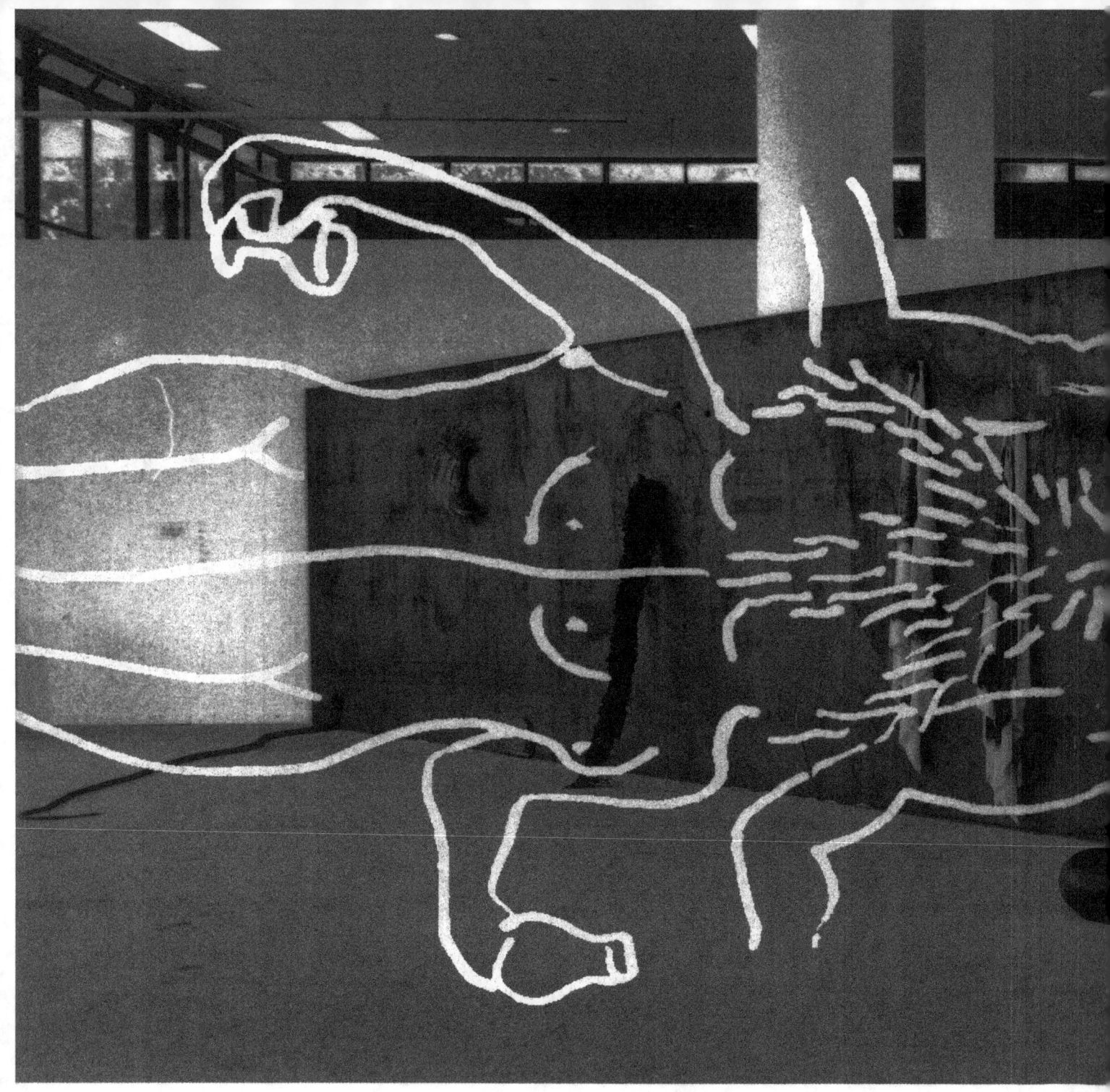

Installation 1987.
São Paulo Biennale, 1987.

CONNECTION WITH THE GREAT TAIL. BATTERSEA PARK; PAUL ASSUMED KURT'S LEGACY. THAT INTERESTED ME. KURT'S VISIONS INTERESTED M
EXALTED STATE PRODUCED HIS VISIONS. HIS OWN INABILITY TO SEE ANY CONSISTENCY IN SUCH IMAGES GAVE HIM THE BRILLIANT IDEA C
THE NOOSE, SUFFOCATED MICHAELANGELO, TRANSPLANTED RODIN, DISMEMBERED PRAXITELES, AND MORE IN THE SAME VEIN.   TO DONATELL
IMMERSION. A GREAT NUMBER OF SALAMANDERS WERE DROWNED, WITHOUT OUTCOME... RAGE, FURY, IT BECAME CLEAR, WERE KINDS C

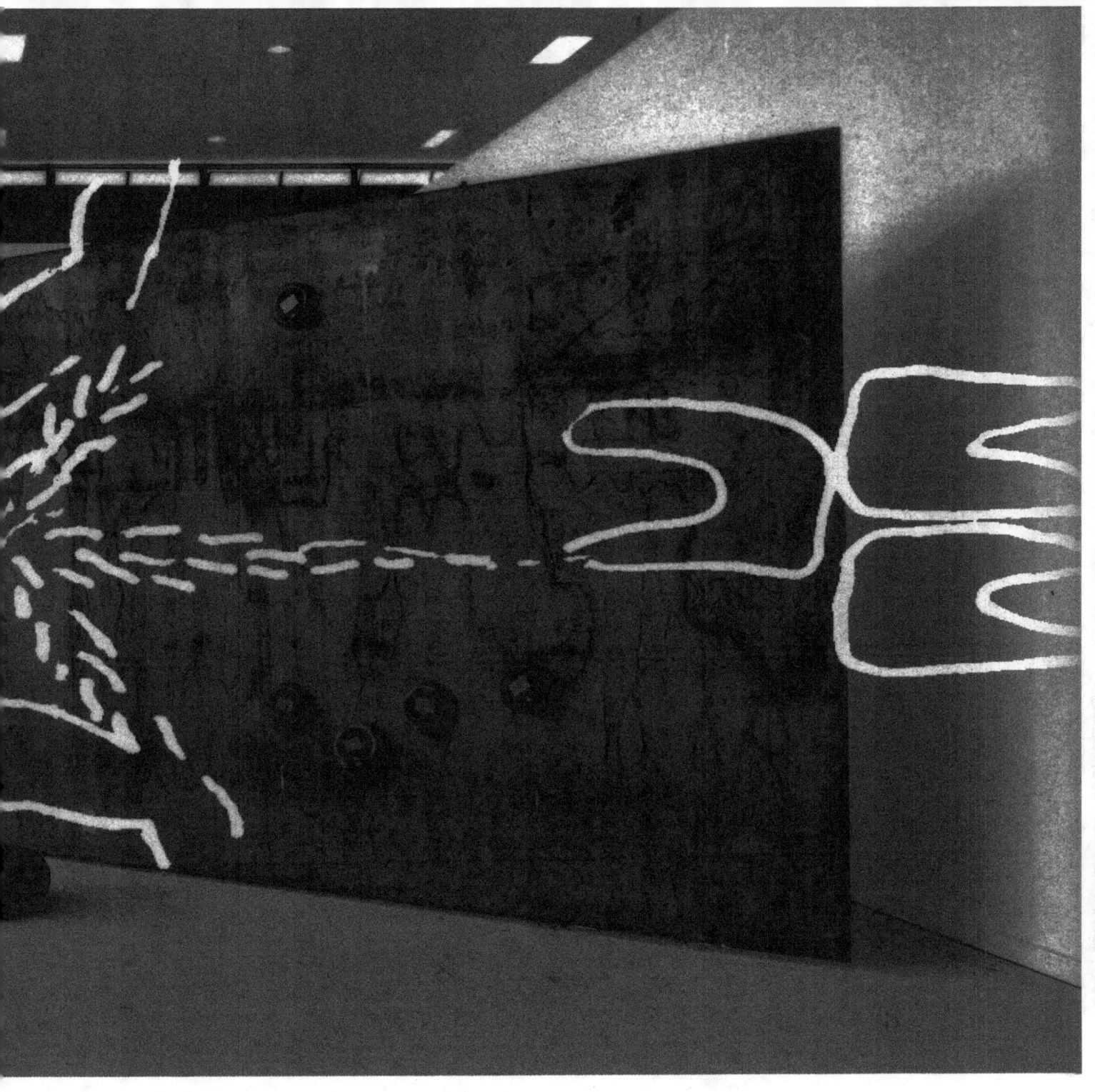

EVERYONE WAS UNANIMOUS IN ATTRIBUTING HIS METHOD TO THESE VISIONS. ALL HIS IMPORTANT WORK, EVEN THE "CONTINUUM HYPOTHESIS"...
TREATING THEM SIMPLY AS BUTALIZATIONS, TRUCULENCIES, OF LANGUAGE.   TODAY, IN BATTERSEA PARK, THE ALBINO MARSUPIAL TAKES CENTRE
THE ATTRIBUTED QUALITIES. QUALITIES IDENTICAL TO TOADS. KURT HUNG IMMENSE QUANTITIES OF THESE REPTILES. THE ATTEMPT TO
IMMERSION. FROM THESE IMMERSIONS FRAGMENTS APPEARED, LIKE RESIDUES AT THE BEGINNING, GRADUALLY TAKING THE FORM OF

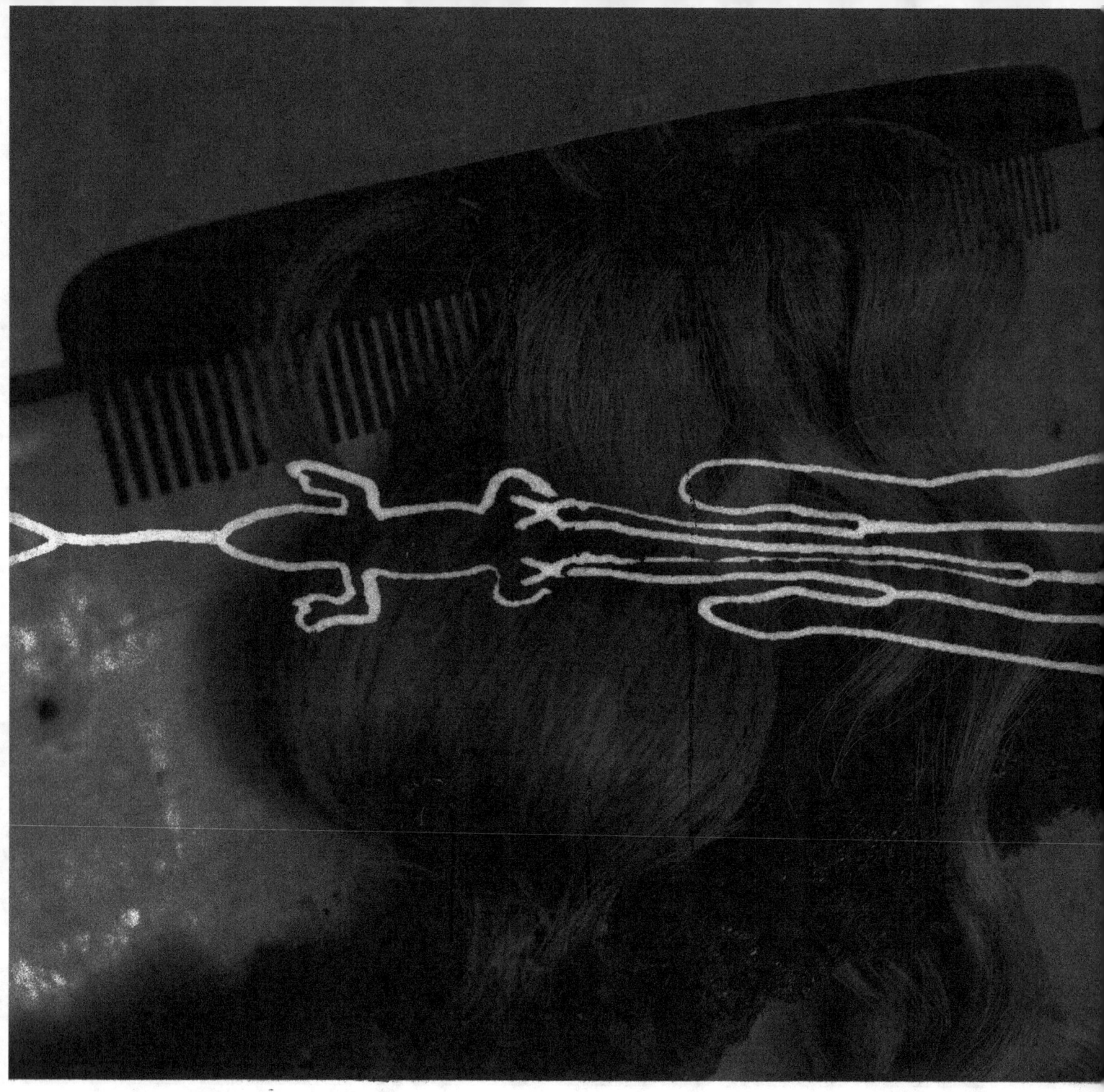

Lizart 3 1989.
Stedelijk Museum, Amsterdam, 1989.

FEW TRACES REMAIN OF KURT'S CHILDHOOD: A TESTIMONY OR TWO, AND THIS ABSURD SECT. NEVERTHELESS, AT THE ROOT OF THIS SECT, PLACE, THE SOURCE OF SOMETHING CONNECTED WITH THE CONTINUUM HYPOTHESIS... A DOUBLE GESTATION?   I CAN'T PRETEND TO BE RECONSTRUCT THE SCENE DID NOT PRODUCE MANDRAGORAS, FOR HIM THE GREAT SYMBOL OF THE SCULPTURAL. AS A RESULT, THESE AMPUTATIONS. THESE SYSTEMATISED THEMSELVES AS A COLLECTION OF TAILS, CHIEFLY THOSE OF LIZARDS. FANTASMS CROWDED IN; IT WAS

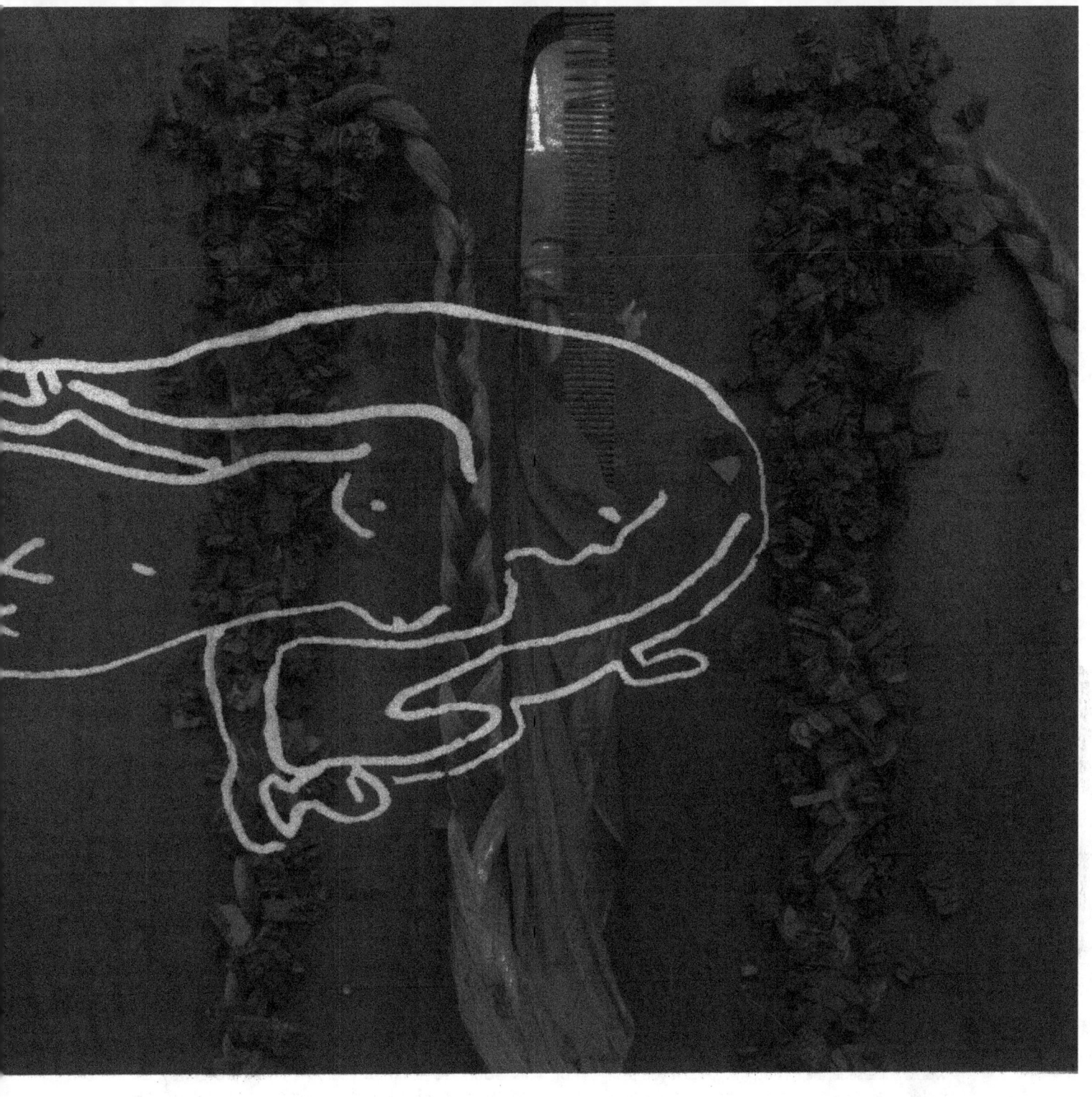

Lizart 2 1989.
Kanaal Art Foundation, Kortrijk, 1989.

OWERFUL ESCHATOLOGICAL STRUCTURE. THAT INTERESTED ME. PAUL ENLIGHTENED ME ABOUT IT, TRUSTING ME, ENTRUSTING TO ME A
ETACHED, MYSELF, FROM THE MATERIAL: THE DRAWINGS, THE HANDWRITTEN TEXT (WHICH I ALSO CONSIDER A DRAWING), AND THREE
XPERIENCES AROUSED HIS FURY TO THE MAXIMUM.   THE SUFFOCATIONS EMERGED SUCCESSIVELY, SYSTEMATICALLY, THE INERTIA OF DROWNED
EDUCED FROM THESE THAT THE CORTEX HAD NOT BEEN DAMAGED. ON THE CONTRARY, IT PRODUCED AN INTENSE CELLULAR ACTIVITY WHICH

Tunga occupies a house right at the foot of Pedra de Gávea, a vast, smooth, precipitous mountain which, like all the mountains of Rio de Janeiro, looks like a single boulder (or a pebble magnified a million times). It is a few miles outside the city. Trees and tropical vegetation cascade down the mountainside and overhang the house itself. Toads and snakes are often seen in the small garden and sometimes venture into the house itself.

For a European to deny his or her fascination with the place - however much of exoticism that fascination contains - would be absurd, especially as it is compounded by the evidence of Tunga's work in progress which confronts you as you enter. A long tress, enormously heavy, made of braided lead wire, clings to the floor. A rude 'club', a conglomerate of lumps of magnetic iron, leans against a wall. The motif of the tress of hair is taken up in an image painted in delicate brushstrokes on a huge piece of fine silk hanging from a string (an image bearing also a distinct resemblance to the force-fields of iron-filings round a magnet).

Tunga's work, which I first saw in his house, not in a museum or gallery, made a powerful impact on me of a strangely double kind. Equally strong was a feeling of the physical reality and presence of certain materials, and of intellectual bafflement. An individual object - a metal comb holding a mass of coppery wire, for example, captured one's attention because it made a startling and unexpected analogy or meeting-point between 'sculptural' energies and those of the human body. But none of the individual objects - each so distinct in its own material presence - seemed to be related to the others. I had a strong sense that familiar certainties, that accepted morphological systems of relationship - the plastic, the serial, the generic - no longer applied, and that these pieces were the result of searching for some new kind of relationship. But it was not a matter of finding a merely intellectual 'key'. Tunga's sculpture moved and disturbed because of its sense of immersion in the physical world, its throwing into question the association of materiality to meaning.

An audacious proposal in early modern sculpture was Gabo's creation of a 'virtual volume' by means of a vibrating wire. Its insubstantiality overturned traditional sculptural concepts, but there still had to be a 'real' volume in relation to which the other was 'virtual'. Tunga would supersede the dichotomy: "When you plunge into water, the shape you make is real not virtual. When I leave the room an equal quantity of air enters the space". How can one indicate this reality? An earlier series of 'sculptures' which Tunga made were formed by, so to speak, solidifying the air between two profiles of a particular person placed face to face (the seven objects in this series were derived from seven women who represent something outstanding in Brazilian society for

Tunga). The solid of the sculpture is that which is *not* the image of the person, but *is* their presence, paradoxically. What exactly is the status of the 'outline'? The end of one body or the beginning of another? The matter is infinite. (The title of these sculptures refers to exogens: plants which grow by additions on the outside).

At our first meeting, Tunga gave me a small booklet. Purporting to be (perhaps really being) a reprint from *Rivirao - Rivista de Pratica Freudiana* (Rio de Janeiro, 1985), it spun a fantastical yarn to account for the way Tunga's objects, though apparently distinct, were linked and echoed in one another. He begins with his own narrative of his (1981) project to make a film while travelling through the long curved tunnel of Dois Imaos (Two Brothers - just outside Rio on the São Conrado-Gávea road), a film which was then joined to make a loop, a tunnel-without-end, "an imaginary *Toro* (topological ring) in the interior of a mountain". And he is led on (or sideways) by the discovery of newspaper cuttings and anthropologists' reports to make weird connections. For example: the 'hair' theme originates with a scientist's report about Siamese twins joined by the hair. After their death the strange trophy of their scalp passes to a woman who extracts two blond hairs from it to embroider an image from her dreams. As she does so the threads turn metallic, apparently to gold. The scalp passes to the Temple of Yun Ka, where the men engage in painting images on silk with gestural brush-strokes while biting their tongues! They were so entranced by the woman's embroidery that they kept her there in a state of perpetual sleepiness to produce the somnolent images brushstroked on silk. This is the origin of the silk paintings (seda = silk, is the same root as sedative in Portugese). There are other far-fetched links (I admit to being uncomfortable with the male/female roles assigned in the story).

Why construct this alternative 'documentation' which mixes the plausible and implausible, the fantasmagoric and the mundane? Perhaps to mock the accepted raison d'être for artistic production which is given by the museum and the art market milieu, by inventing another 'circuit' which crosses the world, time, as well as the anthropological, paleontological, zoological, botanical, paranormal and medical spheres (tongue-in-cheek of course, since he reveals that each of these discourses is as bounded as any other). It could be a way of countering the fixation on the autonomous art object by means of a fable where one object or body is immersed in another ad infinitum (in his story he moves from the visceral - hair, bone, skull - to the super-refined - gold-threaded embroidery - and from molar to mountain). In Tunga's video, *O Nervo de Prata*, ('The Silver Nerve') made with the film-maker Arthur Omar, this notion is extended by the metaphor of swallowing which occurs throughout the film.

Perhaps the point of the story is also to re-examine, or play with, the notion of narrative in relation to other structures. The narrative element would seem to conflict with the idea of a circuit (narrative appears to lead somewhere, to have beginning and end, whereas the circuit is a continuum). Narrative is a thread (yarn), like the thread out of the labyrinth, or like the gold thread in embroidery which enriches the surrounding dross. It also connects with the hair/wire in Tunga's sculpture, which runs in a continuum from chaotic hyperbolic excess to orderly braiding, (an 'orderliness' which introduces another kind of visual energy). Scientific investigation itself seems to have a borderline with narrative, beginning, following up and analysing clues which lead to some kind of final proof (in Tunga's story there are narratives which come through at second or tenth hand, and many things which may or may not be evidence). In fact Tunga's story, as a further complication of the workings of language, plays with scientific investigation as such, by insisting on describing every object or event in terms of others. Is a non-metaphorical language possible, or is metaphor the sine qua non of language to such an extent that science's attempt to describe or know an object in 'itself', and not in terms of another is a kind of folly or mania?

"Thought and language are inherently systematic and fixative, while nature is inherently elusive and protean" (D. C. Muecke). Tunga appears to position himself to throw into question whether such a dichotomy is simply either true or false.

The literary elements of Tunga's presentation do not in turn negate a concern with 'sculptural' problems, in fact they amalgamate with them. What one experiences as the disorientating and baffling element in Tunga's work seems to me to be his search (perhaps only beginning) for another order of relationship in which one body is immersed in another. Rings which are simultaneously traces of circular motion, which are femur bones, which are snakes biting their tails, which are platts of hair, which are magnetic force-fields, and so on. It is a relationship which goes beyond the "inner self" of discreet objects to a "mutual contagion" (to use Tunga's phrases). His sculpture is charged in a particular and personal way by the formidable matrix of Brazilian nature. An energy is running through it which at the present time seems to be always some manifestation of the serpent, as a fluid force linking the primordial with the new space: a *Vanguarda Viperina* ■

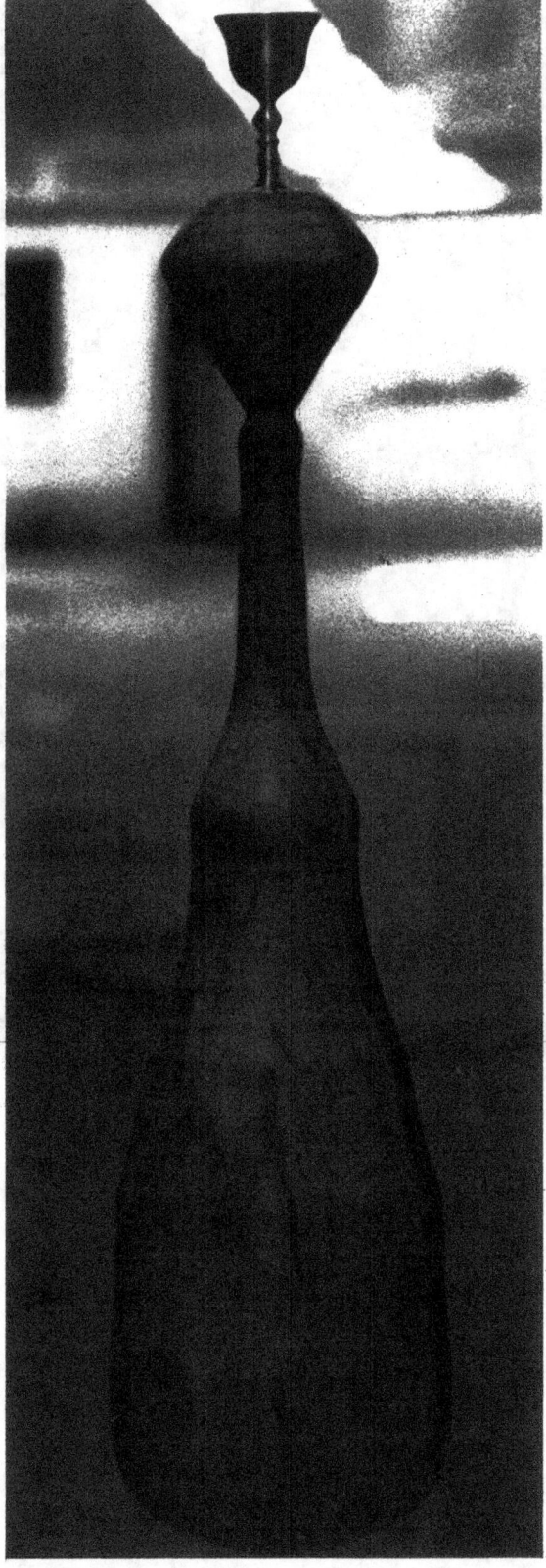

Exogenous Axis 1986
Wood, steel.

Jac Leirner

Os Cem (The Hundreds) 1986.
Money threaded on polyurethane cord, 7 x 15 x 300 cms each.
Collection André L' Huillier, Geneva.

Os Cem (The Hundreds - Holes) 1986.
Money confetti in acrylic tube, 3 × 200 cms.
Collection André L' Huillier, Geneva.

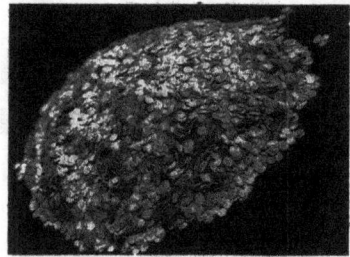

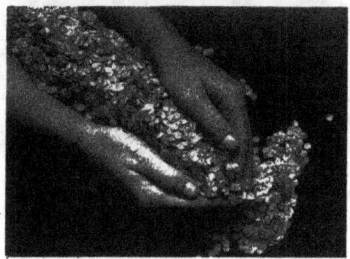

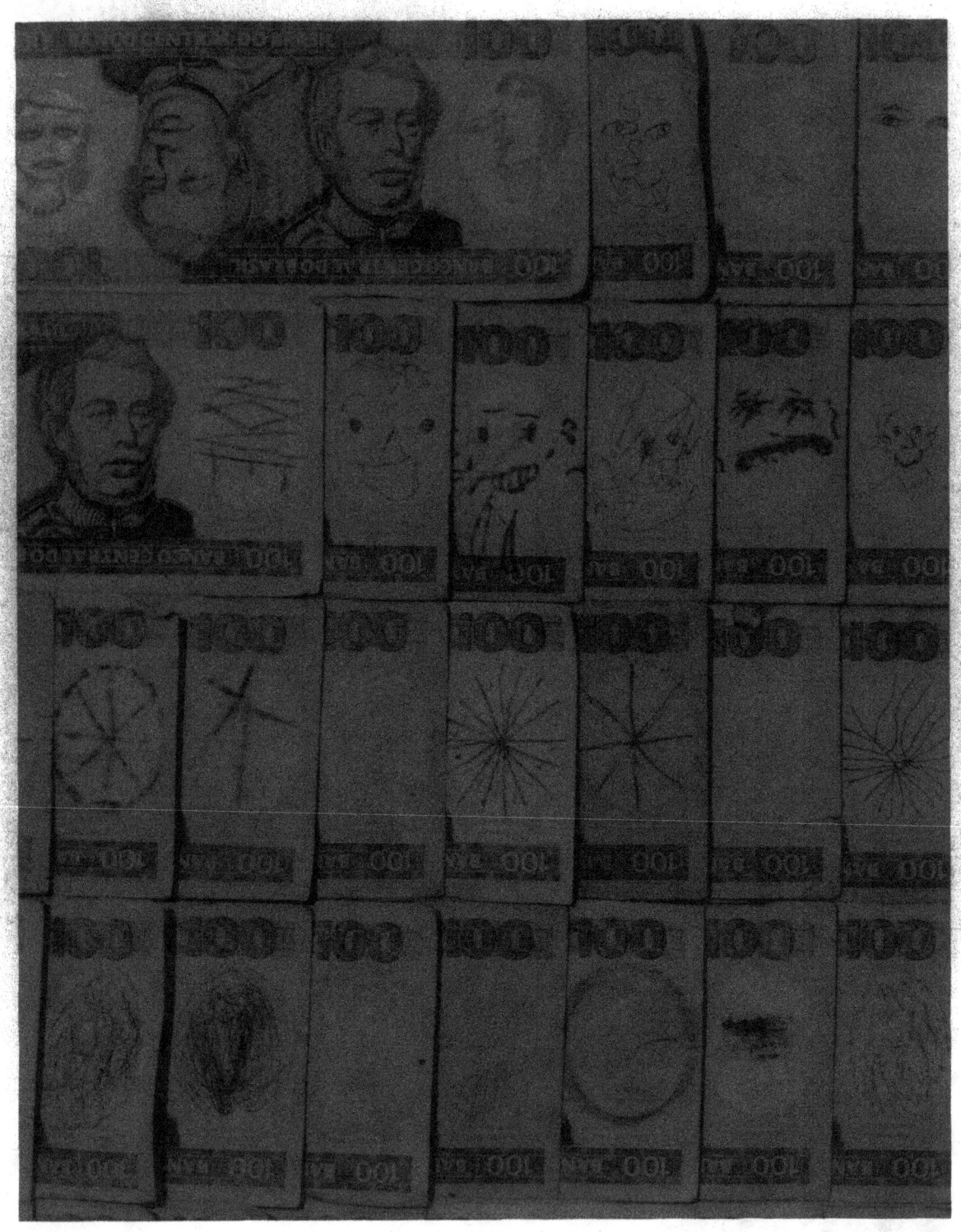

Os Cem (The Hundreds - Childrens' drawings) 1987 (detail).
Anonymous graffiti on money sewn on buckram, 52 x 116 cms, Private collection.

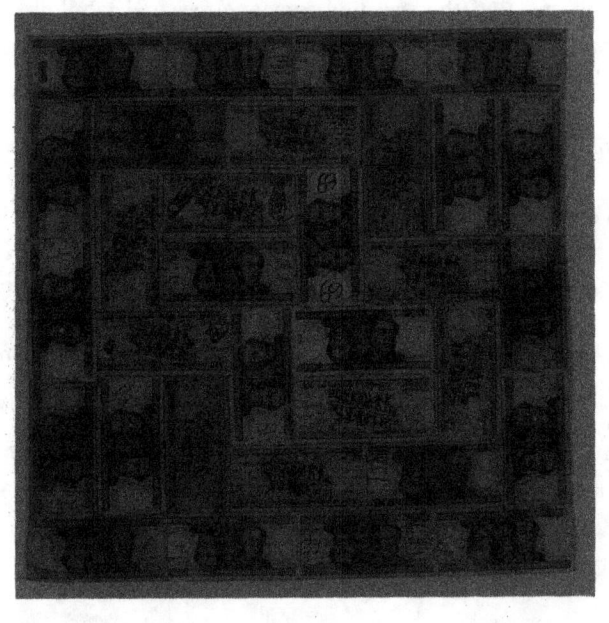

Os Cem (The Hundreds - Eroticism and pornography) 1987.
Anonymous graffiti on money sewn on buckram. 60 x 60 cms, Collection Luiz Buarque de Hollanda, Rio de Janeiro.

First Errors

this is the day that is right for each of you, be ready, the waiting is over, you can make instructions, make everything beautiful in seconds, go and find the way, find someone new and fabulous everyday, black or white, nice and cold, you can see all new models, that's a promise, let's be happy, you have nothing to hide, go on, you can make it, take a fresh look now, you're welcome to the home, come over, wouldn't you like to make something special, a secret formula, a happy year, now it's the best time to eat or to be eaten, there's all the goodness of the occasional breathing's secret, let's go into new actions, let's rest and play, let's drink as a team, you can beat the liquid feeling, you can get it if you really want, it's made to measure for your original skin, it's so fast it'll start to work whether you're a little boy or girl, a beginner, the tallest or the smallest as they see you come and see everything you need, those cold winter mornings in under a minute, the great mountains to treasure and remember together with the real sun, a real fast acting miniature at the end of the other side of the dream, you must rely on it and everything you'll need will be there with a long-lasting effect, this chance gets to work right where you are, something that works very fast, you've never seen a gift like this before, an individual touch that creates superb temperatures for everyone, let's sing it together, it's magic and easy, step by step inspiring clear ideas you can never give up, yeah, bring out the tiger in you, practise lots of fun, it's the new sign, believe it, it contains the spray that removes all kinds of odours and dirt, smells clean and helps you work in bed in a minute or for two hours, it won't spoil your appetite, it's worth waiting for, you see all the one hundred per cent special know how at your finger tips, of course it's the best, you know the way they go for it, you can see they love the taste, there's no turning back, we're in this together sure to grow as a pattern of that new cereal that turns a good volunteer into a natural beauty, honestly fluffy and light, smart owner of every way also hoping to succeed at style in this race where you can still scream for a new face, do it yourself, the whole of the crew will love you forever, with great faith and instinct that leads to the famous treat they won't leave you behind, we've got quite the best of the secret you really wanted, we're new, as you can see, we're all you'll ever need.

First Errors 1988/90,
Edited advertising jargon. Version based on British material, January 1990.

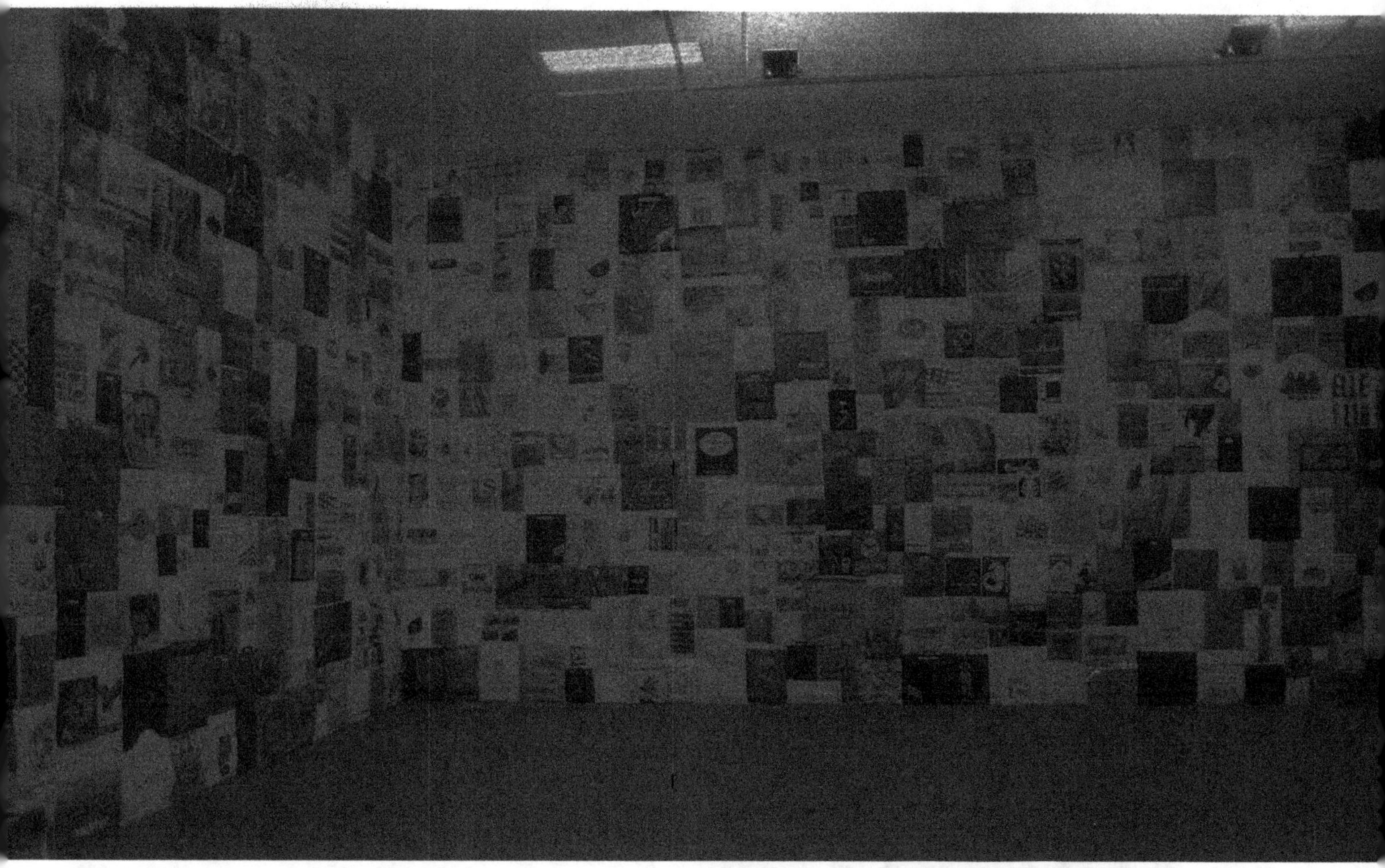

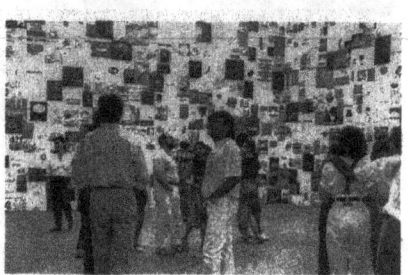

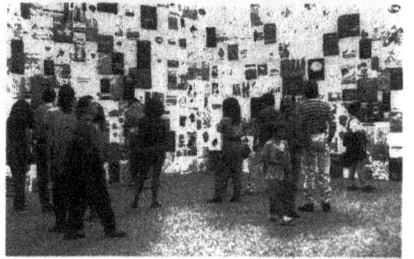

Nomes (Names) 1989.
Plastic bags lined with polyester foam and sewn on buckram.
XX São Paulo Biennale, 1989.

first thought of Jac Leirner's work as sculpture. I picked up one of her long ropes from the floor. The form, the occupancy of space, the plasticity. But no: this was made of banknotes, thousands, perhaps tens of thousands, threaded in a chain. Their nondescript colour, their thumbed look, their dinginess. The object became immensely heavy, lifeless, a parable of inertia (immediately obvious to any Brazilian, but to me only later, was that these were $CR100 bills on the verge of extinction, of being rendered worthless by hyper-inflation). I suddenly realized I was placed on a fascinating borderline of thought. This was indeed a strange object. Why had it come into being? Where did it really belong?

It ridiculed sculptural formalism , and yet its power as a sign, as a revelation of a social and human reality, was inseparable from its sculptural mass. The illuminating 'shock' was achieved, not by reference, by description, by talking 'about', but by simply accumulating, amassing, in one spot, things normally dispersed in time and in space. The rope-like object seemed to embody an insight, an action combining material and thought, of a kind that only the 'visual' artist can make.

The wall-pieces belonging to the same work - *Os Cem* ('The Hundreds'), 1986-7 - introduced another dimension: the artist's discovery, while collecting the bills, of people's graffiti, drawings and defacements on them. At once the material passed from its official level and its official circulation, as an abstraction of social relations, to its unofficial circulation as a carrier of popular desires, frustrations, dreams. The artist began to sort the material and she constructed each individual piece as a generic type: one work referred to love, another to sex, a third to religion, a fourth to politics, a fifth was entirely of signatures, a sixth drawn by children, a seventh of indecipherable marks. The messages were also transcribed and printed as a remarkable poster covered in print from top to bottom, without order and without beginning or end. From 'the culture of silence', a stream of unending utterance.

For her next work. Jac Leirner brought similar methods to bear on her own life, or rather her own life was the point of entry to larger systems, relationships hard to comprehend. *Lung* (1987) was made at the time she gave up smoking. 1200 Marlborough packets (three years' smoking) were dismembered into their constituent parts; each part, massed together, became a distinct sculptural entity and metaphor for the Lung. Together these made up the ensemble of the exhibition. One was made with the cellophane strips you pull off first, another with the foil inner-wrappings, another with the price-tags, and so on. Only the cigarettes were not there: they'd 'gone up in smoke'.

From the poetry, economy and enigma of the action, ideas begin to flow. Leirner made the 'lung' (which we always carry within us) from the ephemeral packaging which we throw away. The units of industrial mass production - like the minutes of passing time, of life slipping by ("I have measured out my life with cigarette packs", Leirner might have said, echoing Eliot's Prufrock) - become the cells of the bodily organ, the dense knotted mass of our vitals, which lacks all linearity. In this way the 'time', and the growth/decay of the individual body - one's own time - is laid across the impersonal time of the massive social system in a startling metaphor in which the physical material is somehow poetically traded between these two worlds, belonging to both and to neither.

1200 cigarette packs were used in *Lung*, something like 70,000 banknotes in *Os Cem*. The repetitive, time-consuming labour involved in collecting, collating and assembling such materials is not the kind normally associated with artistic 'inspiration' and 'expression'. Jac Leirner's is a paradoxical strategy for approaching closer to reality. It involves making a certain kind of intervention in a process which is powerful and hard to grasp, which

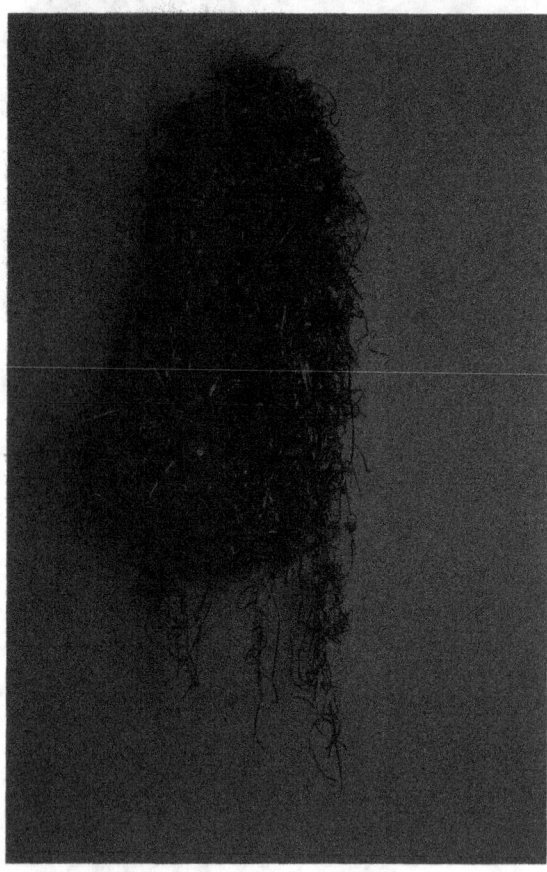

Lung 1987.
Cellophane pull-off strips, 80 x 38 x 14 cms approx.
Private collection.

eludes the individual consumer, just as it eludes the individual, craft-orientated artist. Speaking of contemporary Brazil, Leirner said recently: "Apparently this is a fictional country. Its values are not real. Morality is absent, inverted. That's why I crave so much for the real."[7] Uncertainty between the real and the fictional as a basic experience of the population in a country like Brazil, boiling down to the fictional nature of the ultimate value - money -, has been picked up clearly by a number of artists. Leirner had the sensation, when producing *Os Cem*, that "the banknote is almost an absence" ('cem' in Portuguese has the same sound as 'sem': 'without', 'those without', 'the destitute'). She has since produced a second, or 'ghost version', of the piece. Cildo Meireles' *Zero Cruzeiro* (1970s), and Waltercio Caldas' *Dinheiro para Treinamento* (1977) - works also based, in different ways, on the currency - have expressed the same 'absence-void'.

After making *Lung*, Jac Leirner embarked on the *Errors*. Some relied on a sculptural strategy. *Error in Landscape* (1988) is made from polyurethane cord, colourless and formless:

> I repeated the attitude I had while making *Os Cem*, punching hole after hole, hours and hours and months of mechanical work....I wanted an action which would provoke a gap in my memory, a complex out of time and place, knot on knot on knot (almost ad infinitum), and then place them where they shouldn't be: under a table, at the top of a tree, a foreign body out of place in the familiar and the normal.[8]

First Errors is made from verbal text: a transcription, selection and re-arrangement of hours of publicity jargon from Brazilian TV and magazines. Perhaps it is more strictly a sculptural than a literary text. Whereas *Os Cem* took the very discontinuity of the anonymous popular graffiti and gave it visibility and continuity, *First Error* disrupts the honeyed continuity of advertising while preserving its uninterrupted flow. The contrast between the two discourses is startling and they both, like all Jac Leirner's work, raise questions by merely 'establishing' themselves. Beside *Os Cem*, *First Error* is an 'official' discourse. Knowingly, with ulterior motive, advertising creams off a kind of painless desire from human dreams. By disjointing it, Jac Leirner accentuates the seductive tone in which we are all today enveloped. In fact she sets up some fascinating tensions between universality and difference, since a foreign reader, such as myself, sees certain inflections and nuances - emphasis on the body and sensuous pleasure, the drive to implant middle-class consumerist values whatever the economic level - which suggest a 'Brazilian' variant of a universal process. However, the work is not simplistically condemnatory:

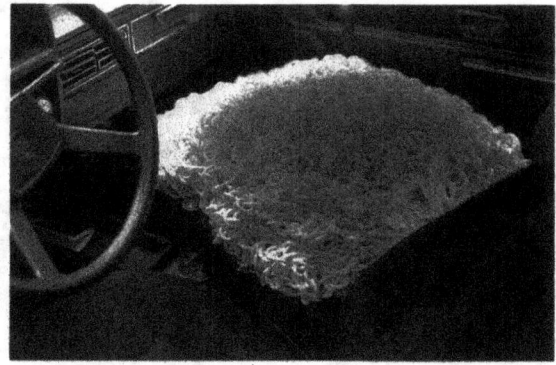

Error in Landscape 1988.
Polyurethane cord.

something magical is made by her out of kitsch, which in turn debunks the self-consciously 'literary' and the academic.[9]

During 1989, for a new series of environments and sculptures, Jac Leirner was amassing plastic bags. Another ubiquity of planetary daily life, usually atomized as small 'packages' in time and space, another ideological murmuring. In *Nomes*, the bags make an environment enveloping the spectator, like a padded cell. This room, if in one sense 'witnessing' the social reality of global consumerism, in all its actual uneveness, also releases a huge quantity of colour and verbal energy which in some way becomes free and available to everyone again as a psychic resource. Jac Leirner employs a 'sculptural strategy', in the sense of working with the physical properties of things. But it is in the word 'strategy' that the important difference lies. Along with a number of other artists today, she is proposing a new definition of poetics, a kind of intervention which modifies the patterns of space and time in which we, and objects, move. A new way in which life can vitalize art, or art can reveal life ∎

7. Jac Leirner, quoted in Celso Fonseca "Holes; This Artist Challenges You", *Jornal da Tarde*, São Paulo, 9 May 1989.

8. Letter to the writer, April 1989.

9. Jac Leirner has made a 'British' version of "*First Errors*", by drawing on TV advertising jargon collected over Christmas/New Year 1989-90, by Angela Kingston of Ikon Gallery

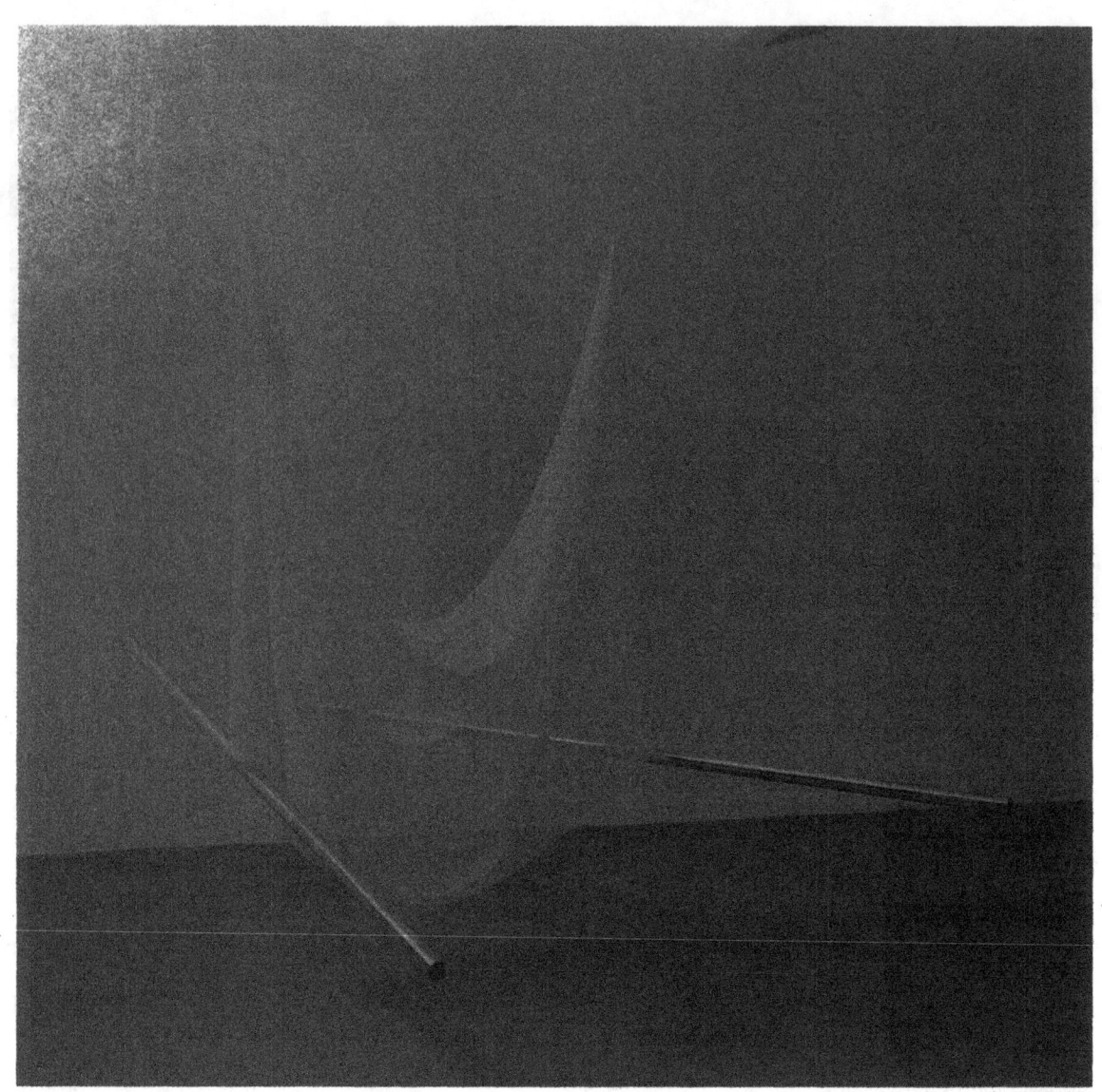

Untitled 1989. Polished metal and veil, 200 x 230 cms.

Escultura Godard (Godard Sculpture) 1988.
Painted iron, 30 × 100 cms.

NOT

The work insists persistently upon being a border. It further insists upon reducing the border it is. It wants to erase its outlines, its very constitution. Erase itself and, again, erase itself, that is the device itself. In this way, it can continue to disregard everything that proposes to define it. Its definition is more and more expressed by the negative. It is neither this, nor that. Perhaps it may not want to be because its being is next to not being. Not is the word that stands for the work.

What other movement could induce these objects to the situation in which they are if not the incessant need to risk the absolute stillness? None other than the pursuit of the most daring and precarious equilibrium justifies these works.

Everything here implies emptiness, absenceness. The work draws its poetics from this singular way of being, from this passion for not being. Its poetics; not its aesthetics—this would be, at first sight, arid and apart. It is enough to see the qualities that the work effects: the emptiness, the whiteness, the transparentness. An aesthetics of desert would be the minimum required to meet these qualities. This desert, however, has its own mirage, its Fata Morgana.

One must be in the desert, accept this assumption and adhere to the mirage like something that does not exist so that it does. These objects are like mirages in space. They are suspended, they are in suspense. They pertain to the world of things having the immaterialness of mirages. They share this being with the mirages not being what they seem to be. Yes, each one of these objects are things, they are materials, though disbelieving, distrusting of their own materiality. They could almost disappear in a flutter of the eyelids; their construction is so tenuous, so precarious, so fragile and yet, at the same time, a calculated, precise, perfect presence. They are structured at the blink that would make them disappear.

To say that the work is only concerned with sight would be redundant. Every work of art presumes this. Though the work has a logic of sight. It seems to be ever more interested in a logical structure of sight. After all colours, after all forms, after all the complex and radical post-perspective experiences, this work seems to be concerned with the simple syllogisms of seeing. But which logic could seeing have, which is the true and the false of seeing, the visible and the invisible? I believe that the work gives rise to our doubtfulness. I even believe that it is constructed like a syllogism that cannot be expressed. If it could, what would become of art? The work thinks the invisible, though aware of the visible that does not exist.

PAULO VENANCIO FILHO Translation by Florence Eleanor Irvin

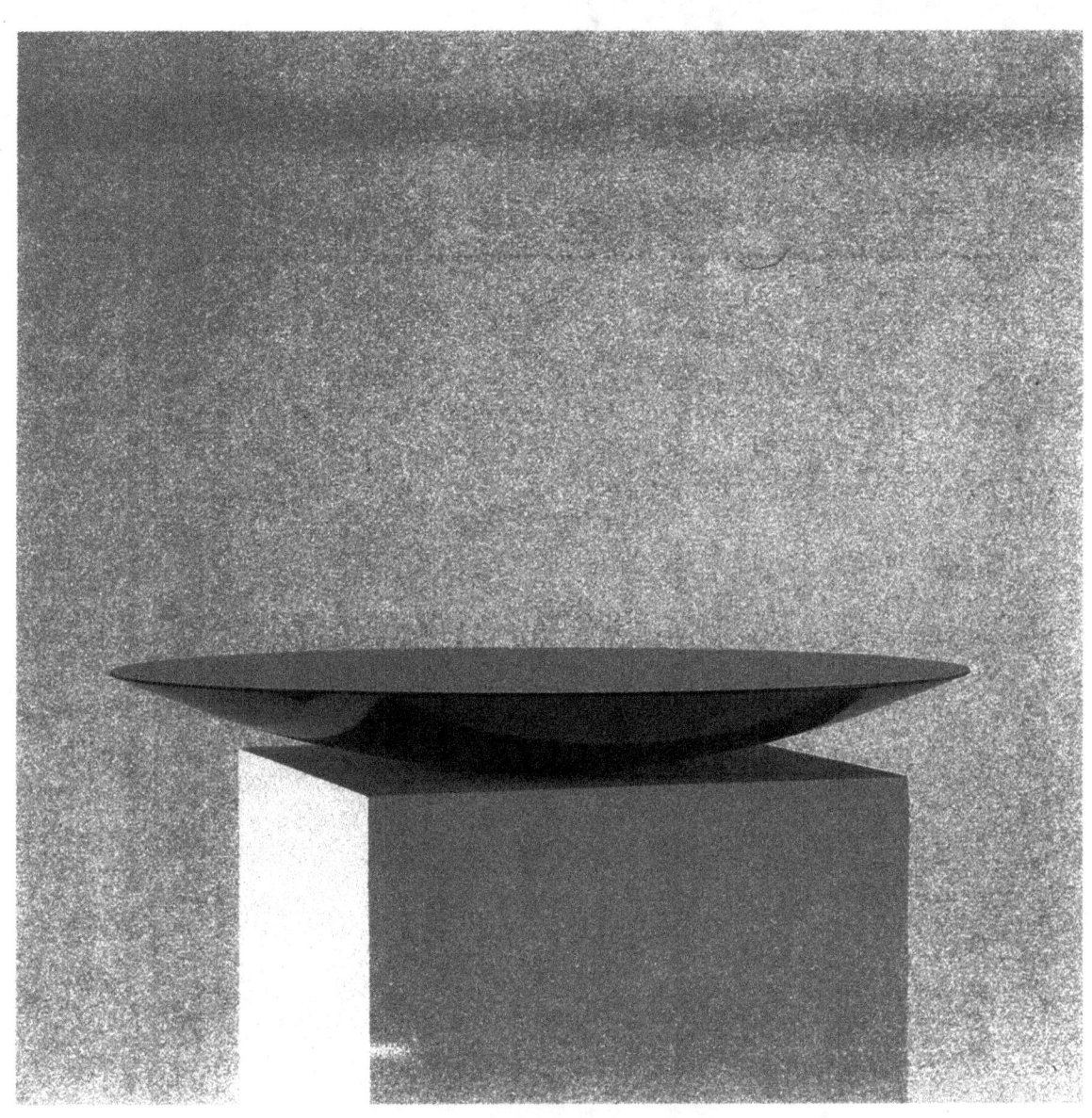

Granite Sculpture 1986.
10 x 80 cms.

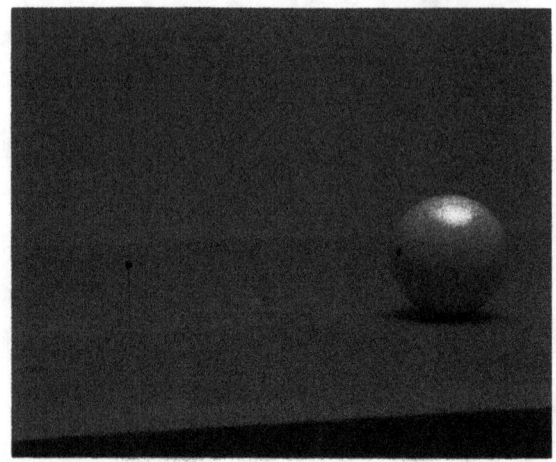

Einstein 1987. 8 x 20 cms.

Granite Sculpture 1986. 30 x 24 x 10 cms.

Waltercio Caldas is apparently the most 'abstract' of the artists in this book, and apparently produces the nearest to traditional, autonomous art objects. But only apparently. Caldas' objects are as much 'not there' as 'there'. It is hard to answer with certainty whether they are art objects, or simply objects. They seem to want to be neither. Caldas creates a spare, calm, pure space. Is our attention intended to fall on the objects, or on the space. Are these simply 'objects between spaces'? Caldas himself has said: "I would like to produce an object with the maximum *presence* and the maximum *absence*."[10]

Waltercio Caldas' devices are again apparently different from most of the work by other artists included here in that, as the Brazilian critic Sonia Salzstein

including our knowledge that this is an art gallery and we are within the institution of art. (To what extent this suggests that only a spectator familiar with the institution of art, and self-reflexive questions, will gain anything from the work, is another question, which does not necessarily have an obvious answer). Ronaldo Brito, author of a monograph on Caldas, has described his work in terms of a strategy which "attacks from within". "Instead of trying to denounce, show or reproduce the so-called crisis", Brito writes, Caldas works from an acceptance that "all that a certain work can do is the problematization of an objective situation that it is not in its range to transform".[12]

Take an early work of Waltercio Caldas, *Perception Conductors* (1969). The two 'conductors' lie in their velvet

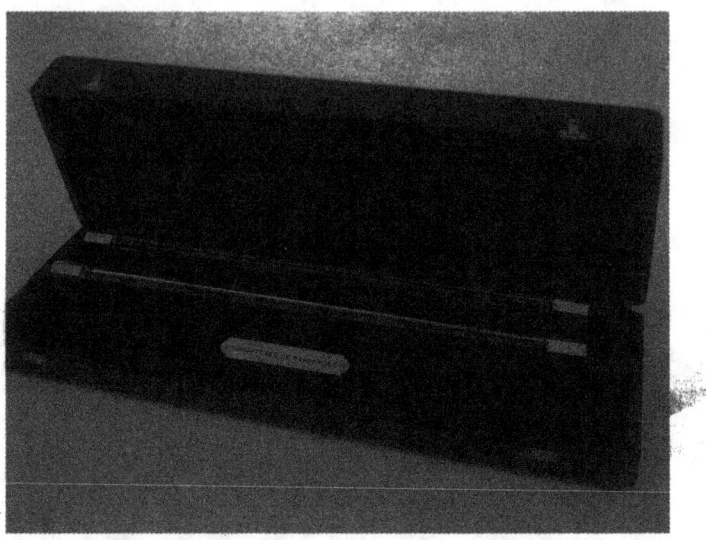

Perception Conductors 1969. 6 x 15 x 40 cms.

Goldberg has written, they "signal their resistance to metaphor". One's relation with each piece "is not exhausted by an act of perception, does not require symbolic decipherment, nor psychological exchanges". "They are perfect demonstrations of themselves", she writes.[11] And yet we do experience them as mysterious. Their deep cool seems to cover, or to be the elegant manner of conducting or demonstrating, a passionate argument intended to liberate thought, one that has decided to limit its battlefield, or its field of enquiry, to the most obvious 'given': the act of looking in an art gallery.

Caldas knows that this is both a sensory, physical experience of the here-and-now, and also a social experience since we bring with us all our mental baggage,

box like the instruments of some fastidious science. They invite touch, they imply investigation, measurement, meaning, and yet they are transparent and void. This object could be placed in a very ironical way within the problematic of 'the body' and of 'spectator participation'. Lygia Clark's propositions (which were being produced at the time Caldas made this object) immerse the body with the mind. Her *Relational Objects* establish sensuous relationships with the body through their weight, size, texture, temperature, movement, and so on, and become a 'target' for aggressive or loving tendencies. Caldas' objects are 'thought' objects. They tend to open up a gulf between what you see or touch, and what you think, which can be vertiginous. Spaces between the senses and the mind become the evidence of their interrelation.

In the way he invites the spectator's imagination, Caldas at the same time problematizes his own authority and authorship. This is perhaps the reason he uses the tactics of negativity with so many inflections and variations. "Beauty is no longer a monument, but hole, production of emptiness," as Brito has put it, an idea which could be related to Zen-paradoxes for renewing the freshness of perception.[13] Thus, by his humour, Caldas is always 'conducting' perception away from its humdrum, routine point of attention. "You would see it in an instant, then it would disappear. You would be constantly re-seeing it. This is a kind of object which it is no good looking at for a long time, which always will be at the exact instant at which it was seen for the first time." Or, in describing the small granite object which rests on four corners: "It seems to be part of a whole which you cannot really imagine."

Waltercio Caldas' objects exhibit a perfectionism of fabrication. But the materials are not significant in themselves (their processes and metamorphoses do not have the importance they do in Tunga's work, for example). Relationships are more pertinent, which is why the 'transparency' theme of his space in the exhibition is worked out through several different materials, not only 'transparent' ones.

If there is a consistent feeling runing through Caldas' work, I think it is that of space. In 1989 he carried out a public sculpture commission in a park on the outskirts of São Paulo. It was dais-like in form, overlooking a valley and far hills. "An invisible place", Caldas called it. It also defined "the relation of my work with the horizon line, the line that's nowhere." Brazilian architecture and art has sometimes been described by cultural historians in terms of a paradox, the "intimist horizon": the perpetual tension between near and far, intimacy and distance. *Mirror with Light* is in this sense an ambiguous object. Most of its surface reproduces the limits and literalness of the gallery space and one's prosaic body as one reaches to switch on the light. But the small point of red light indicates a longing and a deep space. (Or it could be the mirror which produces the deep space and the light the limits). 'Presence' implies the concentration of our attention, senses and thought; 'absence' implies a return to a vast, undifferentiated space (or *plenum*, a word that Sonia Salzstein Goldberg uses). Waltercio Caldas wants us to experience both at the same time ∎

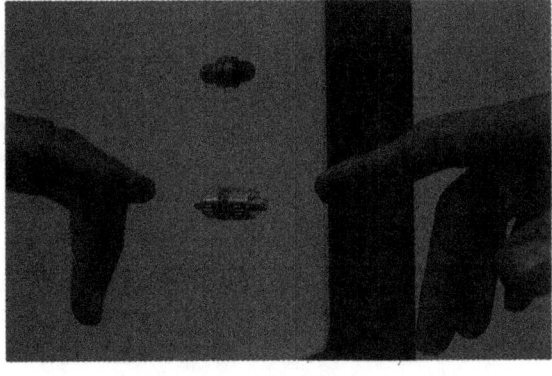

Mirror with Light 1974. 100 x 100 cms (detail).

10. From conversations with the writer, as are other statements by the artist in this text.

11. Sonia Salzstein Goldberg, "Introduction", *Waltercio Caldas*, Funarte: Galeria Sergio Milliet, Rio de Janeiro, July 1988.

12. Ronaldo Brito, "Os Limites da Arte e a Arte dos Limites", in *Waltercio Caldas, Aparelhos*, Rio de Janeiro: GBM Editoria de Arte, 1979.

13. Ibid.

Correcaminos - Roadrunner

To Alejandra in Ostpreussendamm 27 Summer 67

Eugenio Dittborn

1. Airmail Paintings, organised like herbariums.
   Like collections of insects or inventories.
   Like plates in a reference book.

   Fragile, precious, extreme teaching materials.

   Sinking and the pedagogy of shipwreck, of lifesaving and the survival of earlier stages of Dittborn's own production.

   Airmail Paintings which function like boats - folding, compartmentalised life-rafts - inside which can be seen stirring different species, signs, substances, shapes resolutely determined to cross *the disaster* they are plunged into.

   To do so, they concede importance to systematic arrangements, storing the strict minimum needed to begin again.

2. Airmail Paintings disengage themselves from the epistle and the canvas of painting; disengage themselves from the places of their production/emission and from those of their consumption/reception.

   Crossroads of these disengagements: the airmail journey stamped on the body of these Airmail Paintings: their folds, their joints, their creased creases.

3. (In some ways, it is not a question of reading what is inscribed in the Airmail Paintings: brushstrokes, pieces of cotton, feathers, photosilkscreen prints, drippings: more important to read what the Airmail Paintings incessantly *do*: circulate.)

5. The folds dividing each Airmail Painting into 16 regular compartments form a grid with which all the inscription(s) - brushstrokes, embroidery, backstitches, drawings, photosilkscreen printing, drippings - have a set relationship, either accepting the order imposed by the grid or rebelling by mocking it by going beyond it or ignoring it, in other words *playing* with it.

   The airmailness of Dittborn's paintings lies in their *folds*.

6. (Each Airmail Painting is a model of the relation between its inscriptions and its folds. Precision work: either the inscriptions avoid the folds or they pass over them but preserve them, mark their boundaries, un-cover them. The folds marked out like this become a grille.)

   (Are the Airmail Paintings love letters painted in some place of *confinement*?)

7. Distancing effect.
   The folds are distance *in* the Airmail Paintings. Thanks to them, the Airmail Paintings change size and fit into envelopes like love letters sent to keep distance *intact*. Crossing it by registered airmail.

8. Airmail Paintings travel through the international postal network as *folded* letters and are shown at their destinations as *unfolded* paintings.

   Then travel back through the same network as *refolded* paintings.

   Then are shown at their place of origin as letters returned to sender.

   Or as tiny pieces of paper someone stranded on an island sent to himself across the stormy seas of the Pacific Ocean to tell himself:

   Airmail Paintings are Noah's arks, and tents.
   Banners, cotton diapers and scarves.
   Cots and maps.

9. Envelopes contain Airmail Paintings like pregnant mothers contain their *unborn* children in amniotic fluid, like tombs contain *not-yet-dead* white bones.

   (Boomerangs.
   Which fly.
   Hit the blank target.
   Hit the blank and return to destination.)

10. Airmail Paintings carry with them the peripheries they cross.
    Peripheries they cross stamped on their envelopes.
    Stamped on their envelopes in return for a cheap franking.

    In return for a cheap franking the Airmail Paintings *return to their destination* when they *fly to their origin*.

11. Airmail Paintings are a pictorial subtraction. Subtraction from easel painting. Removed they move as pictures *with a minimum of painting* through the post.
    Next to nothing. The strict minimum to cross the network, emerge at the far side and be shown there as an unfolding of different

scarce resources: photosilkscreen, backstitching, pourings, drippings, calligraphy, wool, feathers, cotton, paint.

Scarcity of paint (Oh, that beloved scarcity)
Scarcity of paint: abundance of tiny marks and traces, one on top of the other in a drifting space, one that has always *trembled*.

12. Animal kingdom.
Wool in the Airmail Paintings, travels backstitched, drawing lines and intermittent perimeters with coloured wool and needle on the skin of the Airmail Paintings.

Embroider as travel.
Tiny leaps. Embroider borders. Or disorder them.

Plant kingdom.
Cotton stitched to the skin of the paintings. Absorbent strokes crossing the framework of compartments and the folds of the Airmail Paintings.
Making them bleed profusely.
Bleed as drop.

Animal kingdom.
Feathers in the Airmail Paintings. For writing. Covering. Embellishing. Flying.

13. Between 1983 and 1988 the Airmail Paintings and their envelopes were made of *wrapping paper*.

Because it can be sent, unfolded, and replaces canvas.
Because it can be written on, is cheap and is flexible.
Because it can be painted on, printed on.
Because it can be parcelled, packaged, and is not for letters.
Because it is dark and replaces dried meat.
Because it is light-weight, can be folded, replaces animal hide.

14. Since 1988 the material of the Airmail Paintings has been *synthetic non woven fabric* rather than wrapping paper:

Because it is extremely difficult to cover with stiff impasto.
Because it is extremely easy to impregnate with liquid paint by means of drippings and spills.

For Dittborn , this non-woven fabric is the synthesis between *paper* and *textile cloth*:

It can be sewn on, embroidered on, drawn on, takes backstitching, photosilkscreen print, dyes. And paint only with difficulty (Ah, that beloved difficulty).

So this non-woven fabric is a good surface for the crossing and amalgam of heterogeneous visual practices, greater and lesser, dry and wet, mechanical and manual, domestic and public, well-respected and disrespectful.

Little *shocks* on the non woven.
Non woven: forcefield,
Common place,
The light, cheap, synthetic replacement for a *shroud*.
White

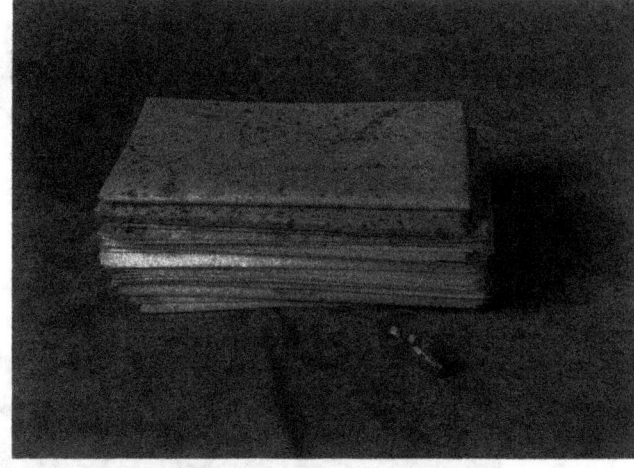

Four diptychs on non-woven fabric folded before being placed in their envelopes for the journey to the Australian Centre for Photography, Sydney. 21 August 1889, Brantmeyer Studio, Santiago de Chile.

15. Between 1983 and 1989 Dittborn produced and circulated approximately 75 Airmail Paintings to points far from each other in the world (most of them in the periphery); Adelaide, Trujillo, Auckland, Hobart, Cali, Canberra, Lima, Berlin, Sydney, Buenos Aires, Paris, Havana, Austin, Edmonton, Cleveland, Brisbane and Santiago de Chile.

On the map of the world, this circulation is like a *giant scale writing*: these multicoloured, multikilometred brushstrokes are paint hanging in the sky in an aeroplane which never finishes arriving.

Eugenio Dittborn, Santiago de Chile, 1985-1990.
Translated by Nick Caistor.

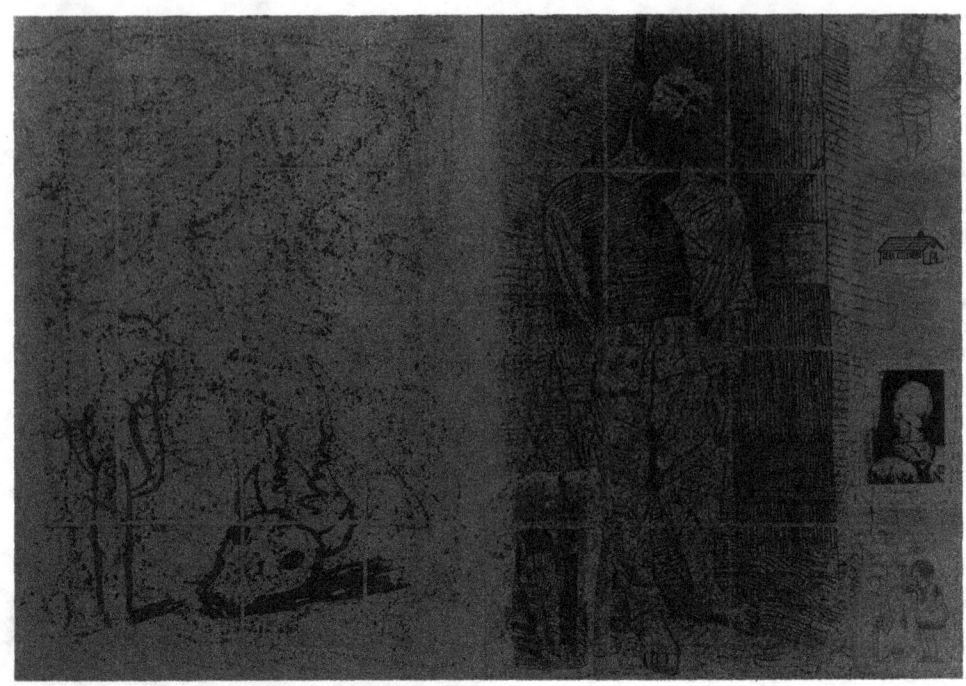

Airmail Painting No. 75 (diptych) If Left to its Own Devices (Jose Guadalupe Posada) 1989.
Painting, embroidery, darning and photosilkscreen on two fragments of non-woven fabric, 280 x 207 cms.

Airmail Painting No. 72 (diptych) The Chinese Worker's Right Arm (Walter Benjamin) 1988-89.
Painting, wool and photosilkscreen on two fragments of non-woven fabric, 280 x 210 cms.

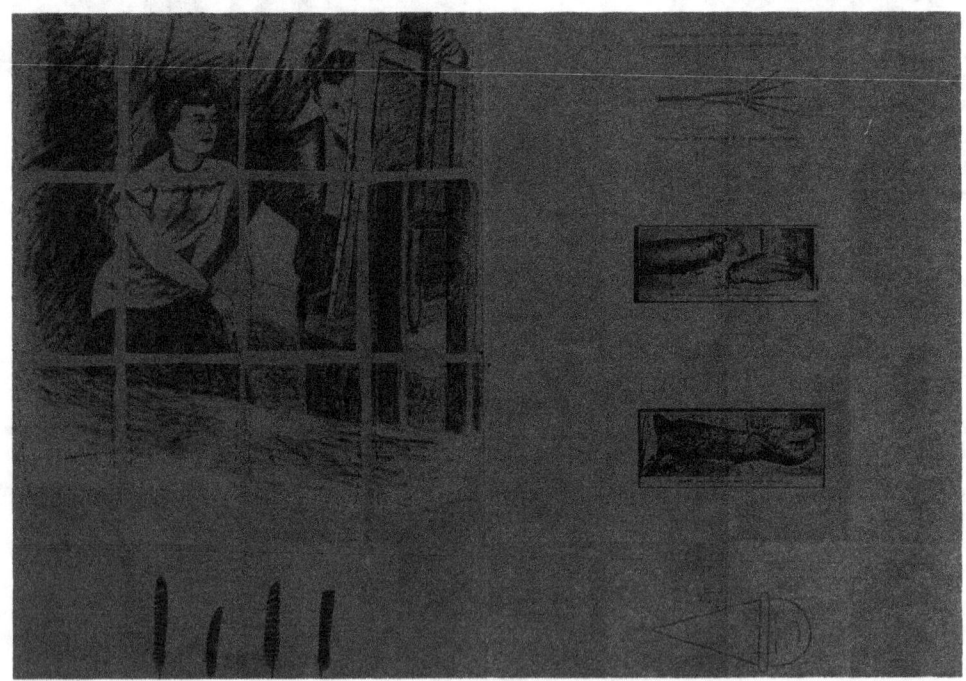

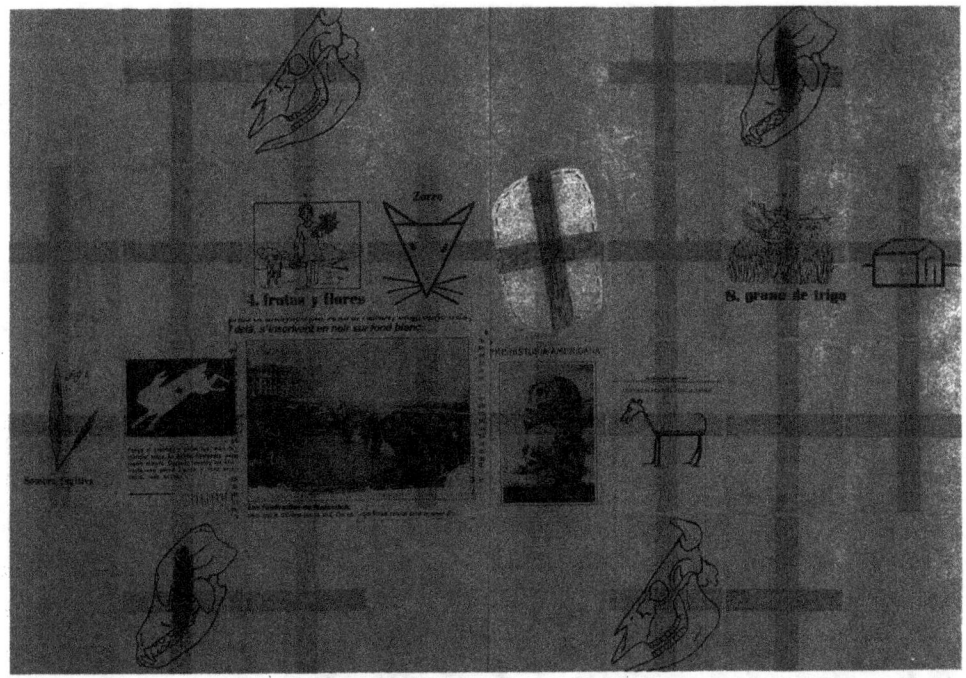

**Airmail Painting No. 73 (diptych) Still Life
(Malevich)** 1988-89.
Feathers, painting, wool and photosilkscreen on two fragments
of non-woven fabric, 280 × 203 cms.

**Airmail Painting No. 74 (diptych) Transcontinental
(Bringing and Taking the Surface, the Volume)** 1989.
Painting and photosilkscreen on two fragments of non-woven
fabric, 280 × 210 cms.

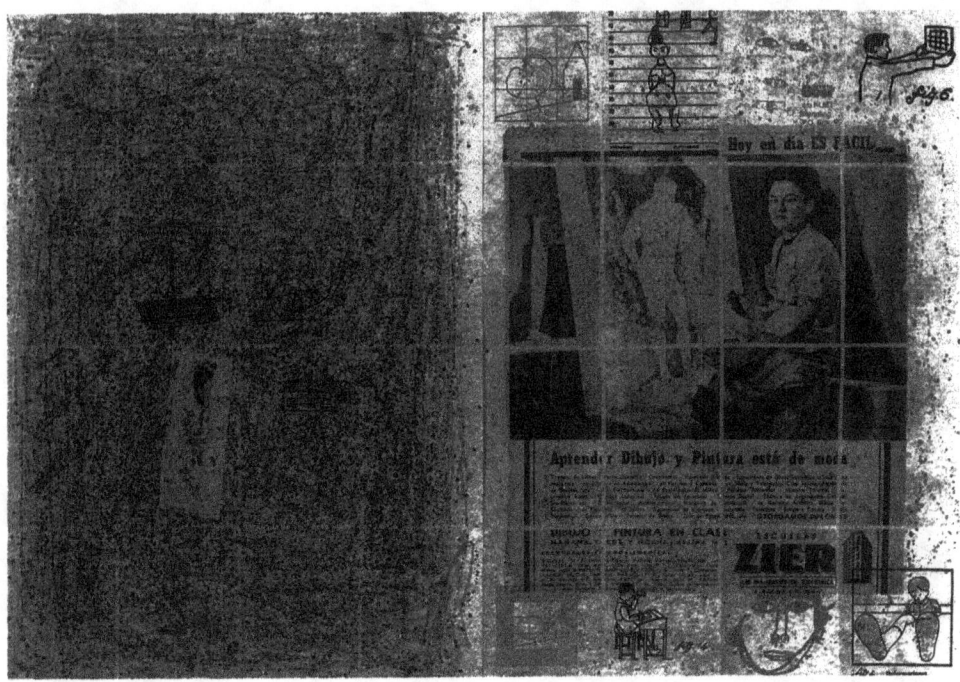

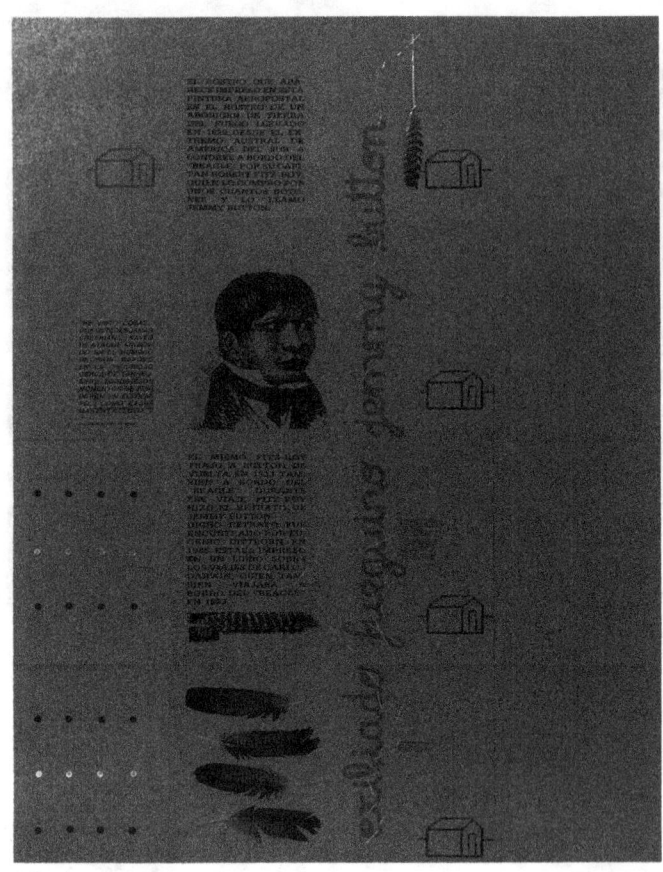

Airmail Painting No. 49 Jemmy Button 1986.
Buttons, wool, feathers, painting and photosilkscreen on wrapping paper, 154 x 210 cms
The face which appears printed in this Airmail Painting is that of an aborigine from Tierra
del Fuego, taken to London from the southernmost region of South America, on board
the Beagle by its Captain Robert FitzRoy, who bought him for a few buttons and named
him Jemmy Button. FitzRoy took Button back himself in 1833, once again on board the
Beagle. During that trip, FitzRoy made the portrait of Jemmy Button. This portrait was
found by Eugenio Dittborn in a book about the travels of Charles Darwin, who was also
on board the Beagle in 1833.

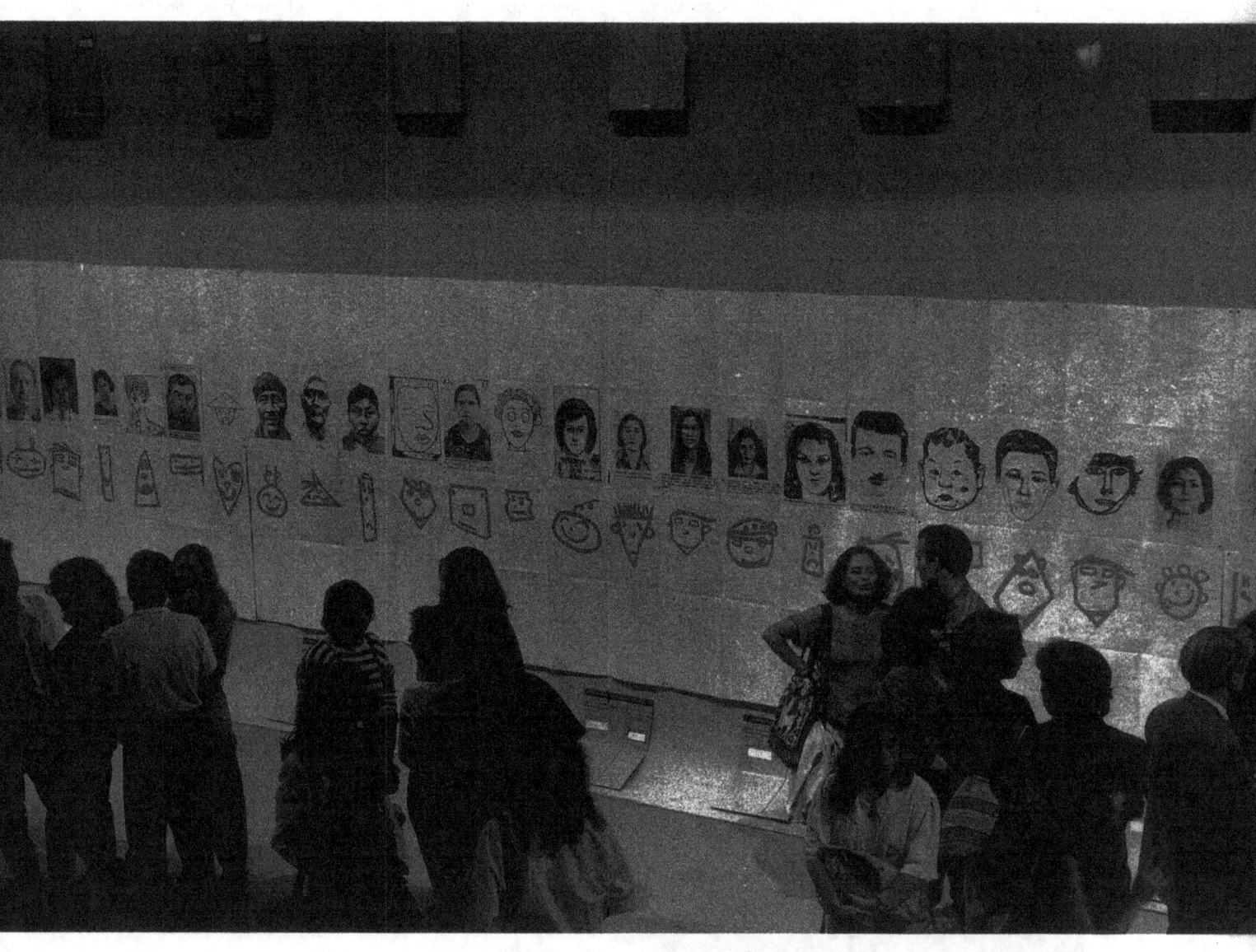

V History of the Face (Black and Red Camino) 1989. Here exhibited at Kinok shooting stage, Santiago de Chile, on Wednesday 17 January 1990, with other Airmail Paintings on their return to Chile from exhibitions in Berlin, Sydney and Cuenca (Peru). Photosilkscreen on ten fragments of non-woven fabric, each 140 x 207 cms. Unfolded : 1400 x 207 cms. Folded in ten envelopes: 42.5 x 56.5 x 17.5 cms.

Last summer, we unwrapped, laid out and photographed one of Dittborn's Airmail Paintings on a street in the East End of London. It contained an image of 'Jemmy Button', an indigenous inhabitant of Tierra del Fuego who was 'bought' by the Captain of Charles Darwin's ship 'The Beagle' (for a few buttons) and brought to London in 1829. To the British a specimen, a mascot perhaps. And to himself? Dittborn wanted us to record Jemmy Button's return 150 years later in another conveyance: an Airmail Painting.

I have had two other sightings of Dittborn's work: once in his house in Santiago when paintings were unfolded and spread out on the floor, and another watching a videotape in London when the camera panned round an exhibition of his Airmail Paintings in a gallery in Santiago. Curiously enough this last, most mediated glimpse, struck me forcefully. When Dittborn's paintings were hung together I realized that he is working with a new kind of 'composition', a new way of structuring. No one work, no part of a work, has any real stability. They are shifting inventories.

Their structuring is new in that it seems to indicate, not a compulsive desire to produce 'one's own' art work, to master one's means, to create a world, but a sifting, a paying of attention to every kind of graphic phenomenon - a stain, a newspaper photo, a stitch, a fold, a graffiti - and one's encounters with them in the course of living. Clearly, Dittborn's interest in these phenomena is not formalistic or simply aesthetic, for the graphic mark is also a life-trace. It is always paradoxically an indicator both of presence and absence, existence and oblivion, destruction and survival. In Dittborn's work, the frailty or persistance of the graphic means is linked with that of the body, the person.

Without superficial expressivity or polemic, he makes us think deeply again about the relationship between painting and human life. This is not a mere specialist or professional matter, since it implies the relationship of the intellectual to the mass of people, and extends to the whole problem of the connection between 'mediation' and 'lived experience'. The artist practises a kind of mediation. A study of Dittborn's strategies in this respect could begin with his invention of a genre: the Airmail Painting.

The Airmail Painting could be understood at one level as a rejoinder, a riposte, to the prevailing art system, and one devised specifically by an artist working at its periphery in the so-called Third World. Made of cheap materials, easily transported, evading the imperatives of the art market, insubstantial, it arrives to unfold and occupy a substantial amount of the hotly-contested space of the cultural metropolis. It also, in the process, refuses to be seen as a floating, neutral, international cultural commodity, since its point of origin in Chile and its journey to another part of the world is exhibited as part of it (via the envelope with its postal frankings, list of previous journeys, etc). One begins to realize, however, that there are other, more enigmatic and suggestive levels of the Airmail Painting.

'In transit': what is this state exactly? The journey implies a fixed point from which the person or object originated, and a destination. It implies locality, habitation, domestication, stratification, sedimentation (an idea often indicated by the artist in his paintings by a small house symbol). On the other hand, motion, travelling, carrying, vagabondage is also a sort of primordial state. The Airmail Painting, as Dittborn himself points out, is only an extension of the first bag (and, beyond that, of the kangaroo's pouch, or the womb). And it is not only the 'work' that travels. The images Dittborn uses are

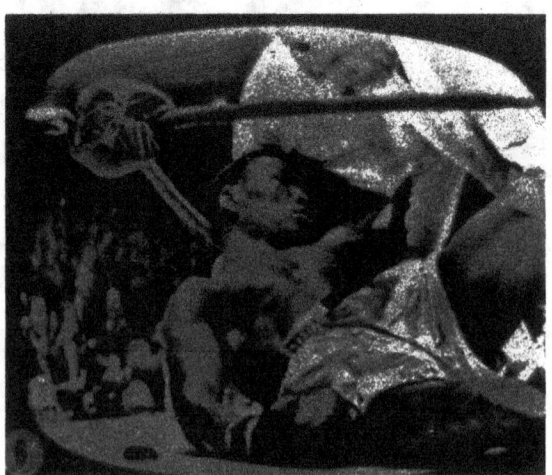

Photograph found by Dittborn in 1977 in an issue of the magazine Gol y Gol of 1962. It shows the agonized body of Benny Kid Paret stretched on the canvas at Madison Square Gardens, New York.
The scene was widely broadcast on American TV. From there it was photographed by a U.P.I. photographer, conveyed to Chile via the same agency, and printed in the magazine Gol y Gol. Dittborn has often made use of this photo in works he entitles Pieta. Two aspects of this printed photo interest him profoundly: The passage of Kid Paret's agonized body from Madison Square Gardens in 1962 to this page in 1990: the successive technical mediations which make the translation of the body possible (TV, photography, offset press etc.) from one place to another, remote and far away. And on the other hand, the exhibition of an agonized body for which there is no 'pity' (pietà). Pity, pietà, piedad (bodies dead and unburied). This version, then, of the Pietà contains no pity.

themselves circulating, and moving between the states of being 'lost' and 'found', forgotten and remembered. The surface in this sense becomes a temporary resting-place of signs which are travelling through space and through time.

It seems to me that Dittborn, in his meditation on the relationship of the graphic means to human life - not as a generalized problem but in the here and now of his situation as a Chilean artist in the late 20th century - plunges to the heart of a paradox, a double meaning. Painting deals with the transitory, the fleeting, the "quiverings" of life, as Matisse said. At the same time painting becomes part of a tradition, a world-view, a cultural hegemony which may be imposed as an act of power (as the European pictorial tradition was imposed in Latin America after the Conquest). Photography too rescues a moment of life from oblivion, but also fixes it in profoundly 'social' ways. All technical advances in graphic representation (photography, video) are also advances in criminology, surveillance and control. Photography, as Walter Benjamin pointed out in one of his essays on Baudelaire, superseded the signature as a means of identification, and was "the most decisive of all conquests of a person's incognito." The whole concept of the incognito oscillates between freedom and unfreedom. When Dittborn uses photos of indigenous inhabitants of Tierra del Fuego found in a book of the 1920s, or photos of Chilean petty criminals from police files found in cheap detective magazines of the 1950s, or forgotten sports figures from newspapers, we feel strongly these opposing senses. The photographic image is both "the material trace of people who have left no trace in the official history of [Chilean] society", as Adriana Valdes has described it,[14] and at the same time the indicator of their 'capture' and subordination.

In a work like Dittborn's polyptych V History of the Face (Red and Black Camino), 1989, 'photography' and 'drawing' are counter-posed with great simplicity and concentration. We face the faces and the faces face us in two very different ways. In the drawings by Dittborn's 7-year old daughter Margarita we seem to see, conceptualised as 'faces', the quiverings of life, directly out-going; whereas in our confrontation with the photographed faces, we cannot miss the determinants and consequences of class, power, contingency, history...

Through both sets of faces filters the materiality of the support, something hybrid, soft and lightweight, and having no connotations with art. When I unfolded this work, I suddenly thought of how the first canvases must have appeared in the days of murals and altarpieces.

Chile's traumatic recent history does not impose itself directly in Dittborn's paintings, but gives a context to something very noticeable and persistent in his work: the sensation of frailty, of "the body's eternal helplessness", to use his own words. It is the frailty of every type of conveyance - from ship to envelope - and of every utterance. The other side of this frailty, though, is survival, which is also possible in inummerable modes. Take the painting aptly called Nine Survivors. We know the title refers to people, but they are present here in several mediated forms: as old photos of faces found in books, police records, anonymous graffiti, and in one piece of text. This last is the statement of a woman, an earthquake survivor, in Cauquenes, a small town in the south of Chile (the periphery of the periphery), as reported in the newspaper El Mercurio:

> "I felt as if a gigantic serpent bored the earth up to the point of a non-returnable unhingeing. I felt, since the mercy of the moment prevented me from seeing, that I was compelled to remain inside of a barbarous demolition. I felt, as after each earthquake in which I have been, the instinctive need to get hold of a living being, which is the other way to become aware of your absolute lonliness. I also felt a sort of emotional catatonic, the fierce sensation that madness is right there, side by side with death, until a joke heard amidst the shadows reveals to yourself, by the laugh, that you are alive".

I have plumbed again and again the mystery of this text. There is not only the survival of the person but the survival of this extraordinary utterance through our bland, official, mendacious media. It is as if it was a statement from the centre of the world, and of living. Dittborn is clearly using it also in his painting as a metaphor for society - for the precariousness of life at the base of the Latin American pyramid, but also perhaps for the absurdity of all hierarchies overlaid on the human, the rightness of all carnival reversals and levellings, themselves little social 'earthquakes' where a cruel but necessary violence is turned into laughter.

The nature of the Airmail Painting as a unique object, following a precise course in time and space, is coupled with its acceptance of the mass-production and reproduction of signs, which is as endless as the potential for releasing meanings which are hidden there. If this coupling between uniqueness and multiplicity is a contradiction according to conventional artistic wisdom, it can also be seen as a key to the dual challenge which Dittborn is making to the art institutions and to the social order ■

14. Adriana Valdes, "From Another Periphery: 17 Mail Paintings", *Eugenio Dittborn*, George Paton Gallery, Melbourne, 1985, p.6.

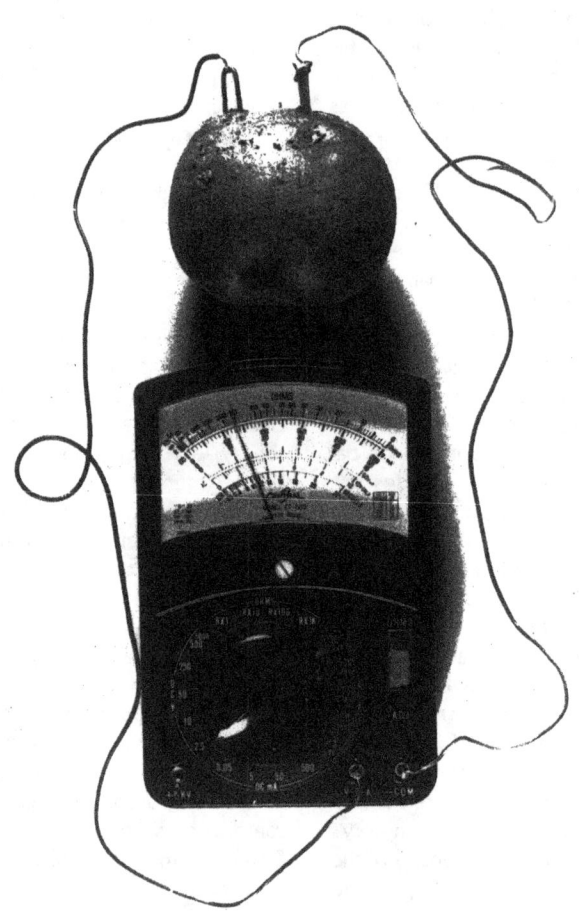

My hope is that this work will trace a clear line from the tripod where my father performed his Sunday tasks to the cooking pot where my mother stirred the food (both of them working with fire and nourishment, with a world that needed to be observed, transformed, kept, or distributed). "Eaters of garlic and onion" (and potatoes), they forced their will upon a problematic, imperious reality which perhaps shaped my own line of work; it may be that all I have done is to convey the feeling they transmitted to me. But a ceaseless clarity informed my curiosity, my search for a meaning: a path out of darkness towards a glimmer of light.

Unconsciously then, I began to articulate symbols: man's foodstuffs, energy, the rose, things losing stability and the transformations this causes, so that I began making my contribution to the fire of renewal which does not necessarily mean change, unless it is combined with an awareness of what can be preserved.

Those of us from an immigrant race have always found the landscape confronting us to be too small. Kept from any knowledge of what was near at hand, we wanted more, and what we find around us is not enough. That was why the symbol of the lamp replaced that of any calm, natural path.

In our work there is either imitation, in those of us who are skilful, or hypotheses which reach out beyond what our immediate surroundings appear to offer.

We are entering a period when the circumstances of reality are being controlled; a country in disorder, "promised land", will discover its way forward in a twofold vision: outside-inside, which must surely find their point of stability.

Victor Grippo 1988
Translated by Nick Caistor

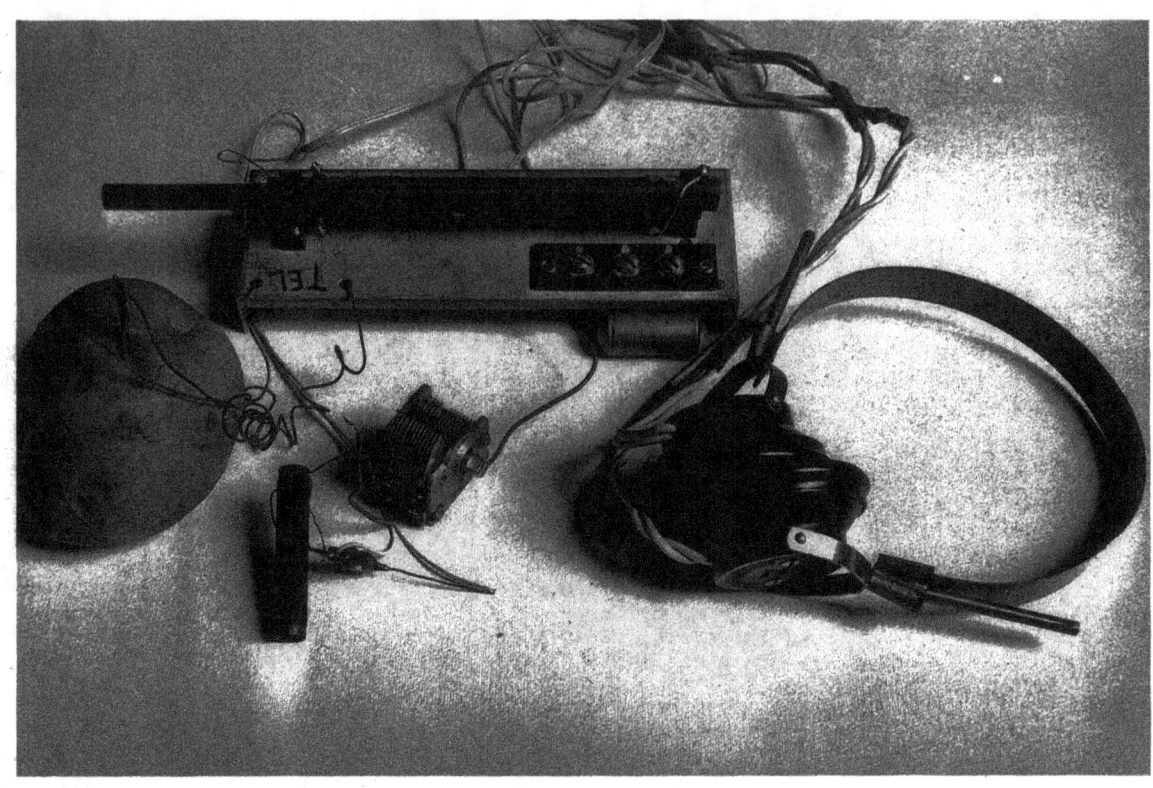

Potato powered radio 1973.

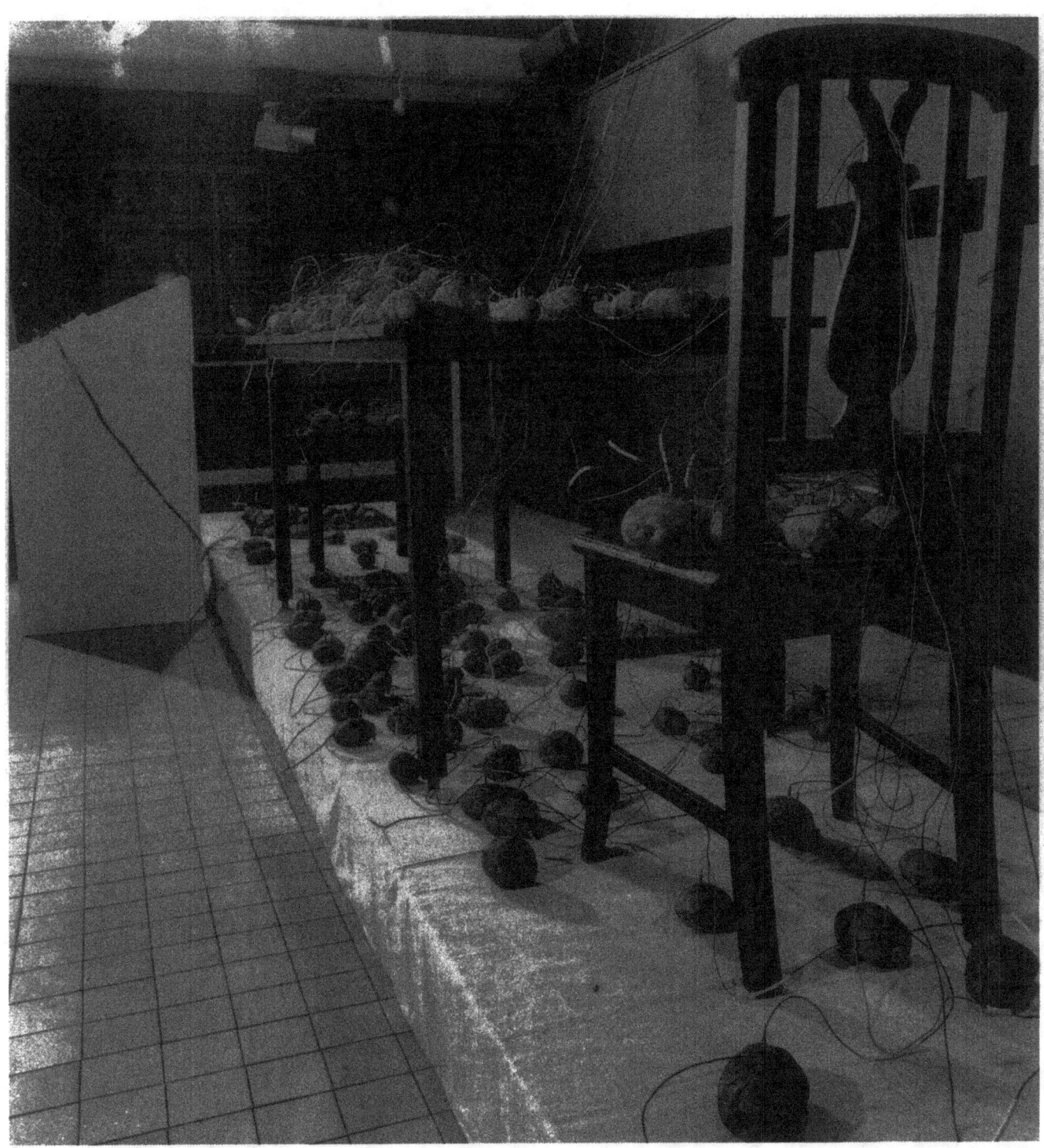

Analogy I (variation) 1976.
Potatoes, wire, electrodes, voltmeter, text.
CAYC, Buenos Aires, 1976.

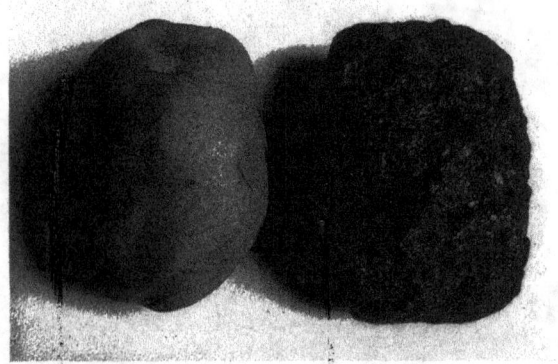

Synthesis 1973.
Potato, stone.

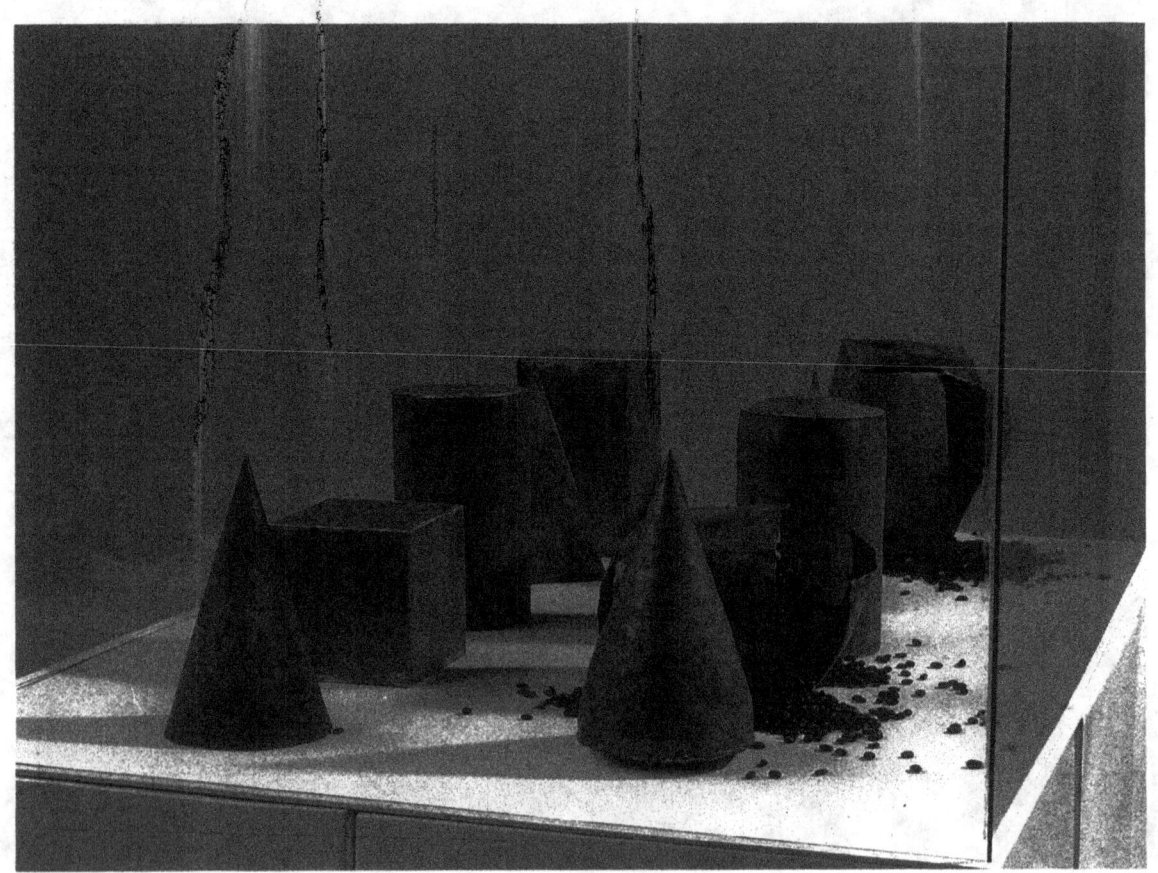

Life - Death - Resurrection 1980.
Lead, beans, water, h20 cms

Board 1978.

The sight of a room full of potatoes, scattered over low platforms, on tables and chairs, each one manifesting its small charge of electricity (0.7 volts) along wires which run to a common console, has lost none of its impact, either aesthetic or didactic, since Victor Grippo first proposed it at the end of the '60s. This work has something of the metaphors of self-renewing energy found in kinetic art (e.g. David Medalla's *Bubble Machines*, certain works of Takis and Soto), something of the direct materiality associated with Joseph Beuys and others, and something of those works which lay out in space the

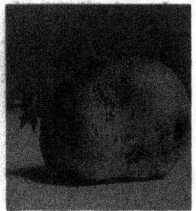

results of an investigation. But the particular combination of the discourses of art, science, and of everyday existence, is very much Grippo's own. The potatoes themselves constantly renew the complex of metaphors: as Grippo says, with only a little licence, in this world "there is no day without potatoes".[15]

Rather than a linear evolution, Grippo's work seems to show the result of a prolonged meditation around a series of *Analogies*. First and most obvious: that between art and science. With a penchant for experimentation from childhood, and training as a chemist, Grippo has always worked on the assumption of some kind of lost unity between science and art: "If we can speak of a scientific law or experiment as having beauty, then we can speak of art as containing, in its own way, a natural law."[16] Analogies between these two kinds of knowledge spread out to incorporate other traditional oppositions: those between the tools of labour and artistic objects, between material and consciousness, between the natural and the artificial, between the erudite and the popular, between didactic and poetic expression. Study of these analogies would lead one beyond the compartmentalised and literal towards a "renovation in the field of aesthetics".

A distinction between 'scientific' and 'emotive' language was known to the earliest rhetoricians. As a device of communication, Grippo's works seem to play very profitably with this dichotomy. We are at first surprised to discover that potatoes do indeed contain electricity, at the same time to feel them as a sign of overwhelming historical and human realities. It is a cool poetics: the passionate things Grippo has to say are communicated with the matter-of-factness of a technical

demonstration. In the potato installation, the whole configuration of objects in space denotes energy:

> It is a question of making evident the energy in the image. For this I took the most commonplace and ordinary object which would have those properties, something you see all the time. An object you see without seeing it, which you use without knowing it contains energy, something which is around all the time: the potato. Besides, the potato originates in Latin America (in the North of Argentina, in Peru and Bolivia). It's in every

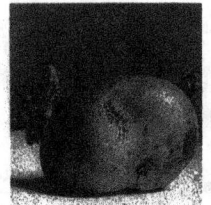

> kitchen in the world, the cheapest foodstuff.
> It's strange, now I think about it, that I've always been intrigued by the potato - since I was a kid. I once made a radio which was powered by a potato that I'd pinched from my mother. Years later this little thing, this toy, became a kind of pedagogical work to make a source of energy visible in an unexpected way.[17]

The electrical energy is the analogy or metaphor: for consciousness, for the repressed potential of the Latin American peoples. Or possibly for 'voice'. The Argentinian critic Jorge Glusberg has pointed out how many popular sayings and expressions there are around Buenos Aires which use "papa".[18] In this net of relationships Grippo would like to seek connections which have been lost, where in a sense the potato 'leads' human consciousness. He mentions an experiment:

> Pieces of potato, hermetically sealed in glass vessels, in an oxygen atmosphere, at constant pressure and temperature, produce, 48 hours ahead, a metabolic curve on the graph which is the inverse of the coming change in the surrounding barometric pressure. Science does not know the reason for this phenomenon. The potato 'knows'. Man can 'know'.[19]

It is known that the Incas made links between brain trepanation and the cultivation of new varieties of potato. Of course such connections may or may not be taken literally, but for Grippo these reports signal the probable loss of knowledge which was inseparable from religion and therefore swept away by the Conquistadors' Christianity. Methodologies which integrate art, science and religion are interesting to him for the possibility they have to "renovate" the field of aesthetics today, by promoting a "convergence" of human experiences as an antidote to fragmentation. Grippo warns, however, of the danger of a folkloric attitude towards Latin America. There is nothing folkloric in his own work. It does, however, have considerable rapport with the *artisanal*.

Analogy IV (1972) (see p.21) refers to the domestic scene, to a humble table. It is perhaps a way to give a basis in the common everyday experience to a sophisticated play of opposites. The white and black

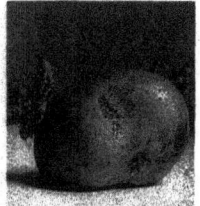

halves of the table, the 'real' place-setting with potatoes and the transparent acrylic version, make a subtle and succinct confrontation: positive/negative, natural/artificial, present/absent, material/metaphor. This table has a companion in another table which Grippo put on show in 1978, *Board*, where the enigmatic borderline between useful object and poetic object, and therefore between life and art, is dramatised by the most humdrum means. This was a table with the traces of everyday use - writing, dough-making, mending a watch, eating, drinking, crying - focussed by a text running over its skin. A written table? Tabled writing? An object as the convergence of multiple experiences.

The artisanal references could be seen as an artist's

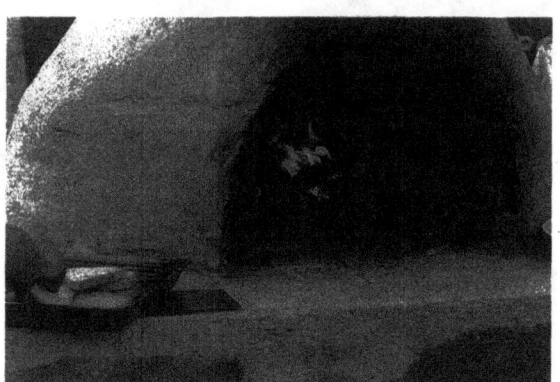

Victor Grippo, Jorge Gamarra and Rossi (a rural worker). Popular rural oven, with bread baked and handed out to passers-by. Built September 23, 1972 in Plaza Roberto Arlt, Buenos Aires, as part of the exhibition *Art and Ideology* organized by CAYC. Destroyed September 25, 1972 by order of the municipal Head of Culture.

response to imperfect and uneven modernization in a country like Argentina. The rural earth oven which Grippo arranged to have constructed in a new public square in Buenos Aires in 1972, with bread baked and handed out to passers-by as an event, dramatised, as Jorge Glusberg pointed out, the polarization between city and country in Argentina (one third of the population live in the capital: these disparities are increasing throughout most of Latin America) and the simultaneous existence of ancient and modern.[20] This contradiction, and all the tensions between possibility and waste, would seem to

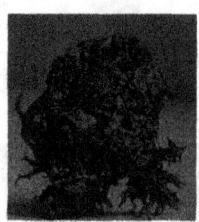

be an essential factor in Grippo's witness to an environmental/human 'energy'. Another, more recent, *Analogy* of his is the *Life - Death - Resurrection* series. Ordinary beans, mixed with water, split open the geometrical lead solids which contain them. Typical of Grippo here again is the modest presence of the material itself, the absence of any sort of expressive rhetoric, to demonstrate the tremendous power of the 'pulse'.

"The work of art is more than a product, it must be evidence of a transformation of things, of people, of the artist."[21] ■

15. Quoted in Jorge di Paola, "Victor Grippo: Cambiar los Habitos, Modificar la Conciencia", *El Porteño* No 4, Buenos Aires, 1982.

16. Quoted in Jorge Glusberg, *Victor Grippo*, Art Criticism Briefs, AICA Argentinian Section, Buenos Aires.

17. Jorge di Paola, op. cit.

18. Jorge Glusberg, op. cit.

19. Letter to the writer, 1975.

20. Jorge Glusberg, op. cit.

21. Jorge di Paola, op. cit.

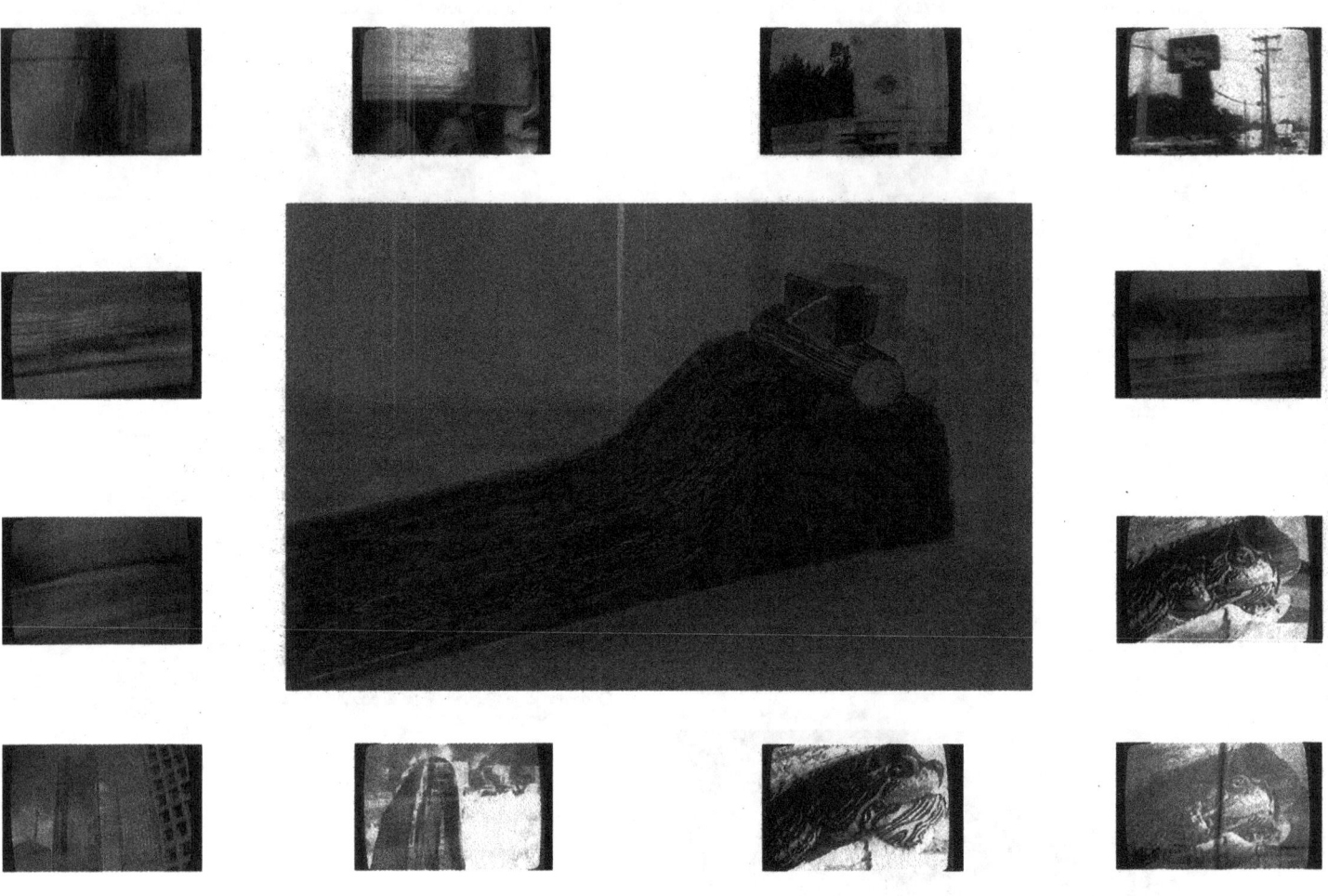

Anakonda 1989.
Drawing for video installation, red fake snake skin, dirt mound, tree trunk, TV monitor, red mirror plastic on wall, approx 274 × 457 × 137 cms.
Stills from the videotape.

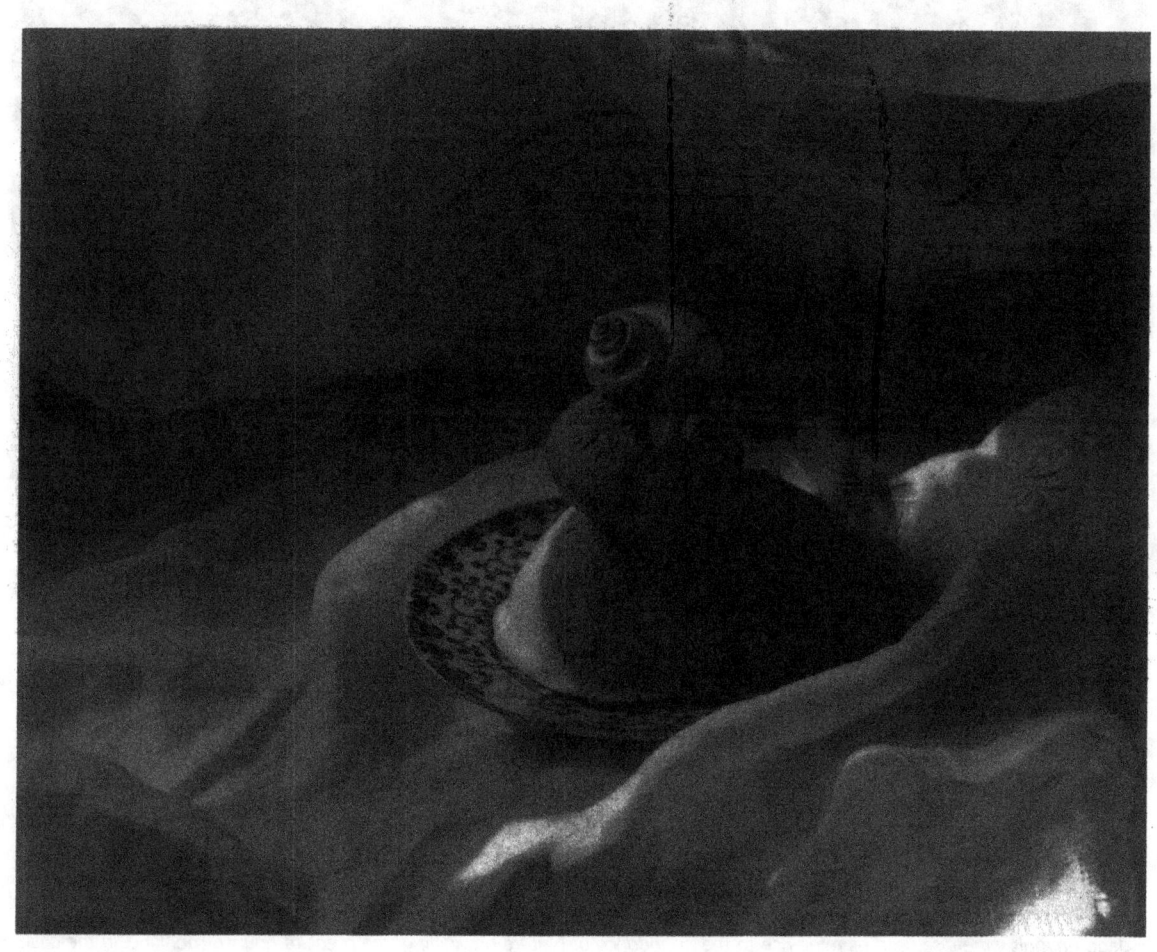

Nature Morte 1987.
Black and white print 36 x 45 cms.

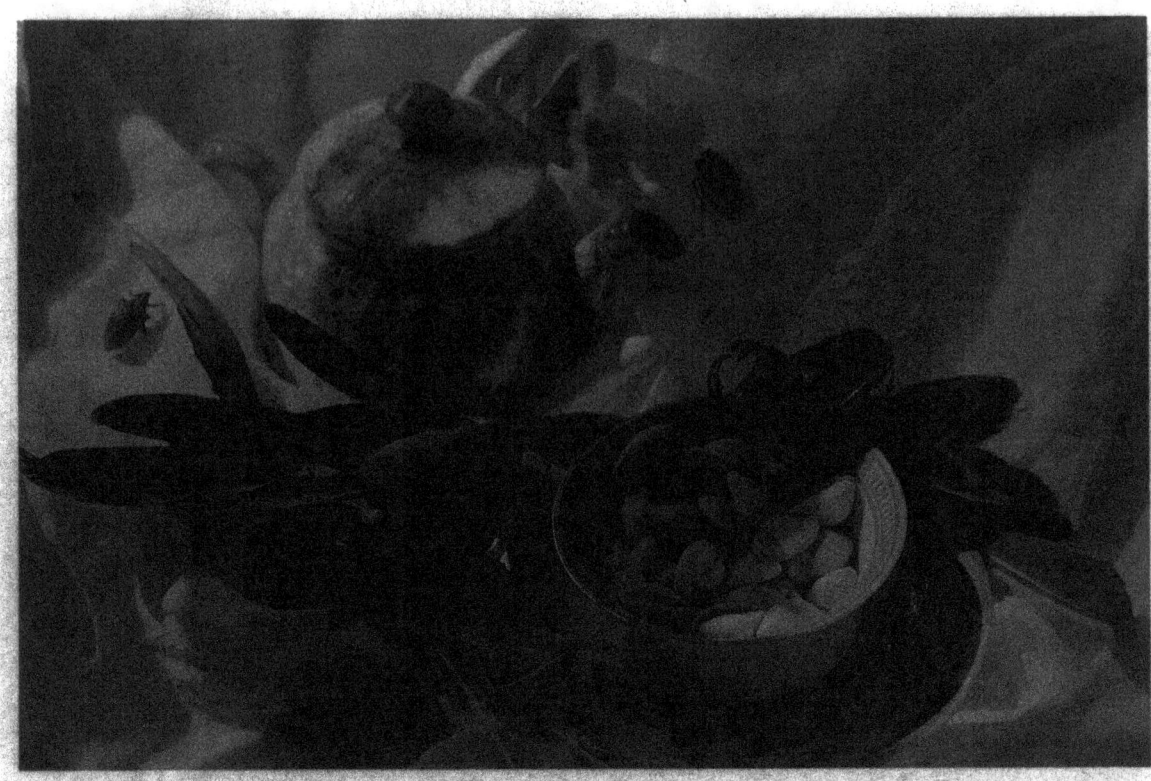

Nature Morte 1989.
Cibachrome print, 31 x 48 cms.

Nature Morte

Nature Morte in French means 'Still Life' but also 'Dead Nature'.

In this Cibachrome series I am working with the concept of Still Life and also with ecological ideas. Thus, the French title works as a 'jeux de mots' (play of words).
The intention of working with natural light is to bring in the Flemish tradition of still life painting to my photos. In that tradition, dead animals were also used as reference to the abundance of Nature providing game meat to nourish mankind. In the case of my work, I use bones, furs and feathers more as leftovers, drifts of an ecological decimation. And the linen, elegant china and silverware I use as a metaphor for the "sophistication" of our culture nourished from this macabre banquet.
This banquet is so well camouflaged and done with such complacency that it denies us to be in touch with our own psychotic morbidity.
It is almost as if we are losing the desire for survival as a species by destroying not only the ecological system around us but also our companions of the animal kingdom without clemency or compassion but with a decadent perversity.

Regina Vater

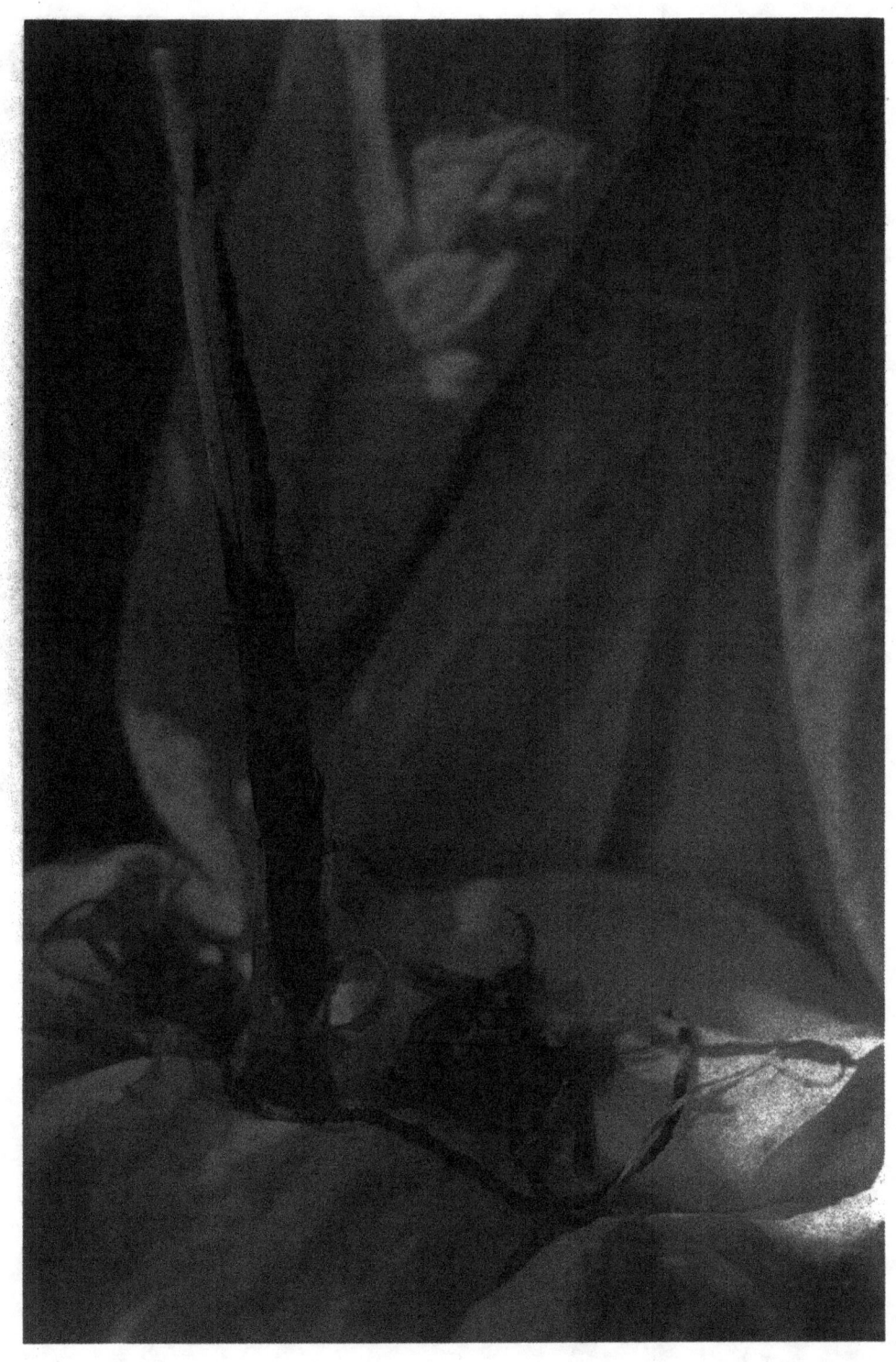

Nature Morte 1989.
Cibachrome print, 31 × 48 cms.

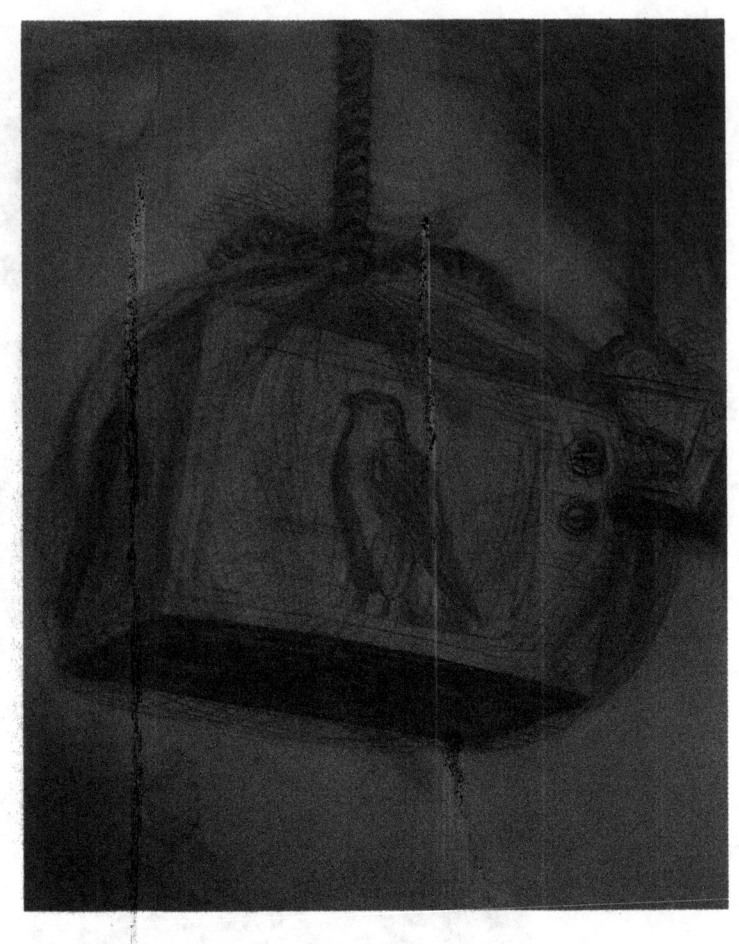

Nature 1989.
Drawing for video installation, 4/5 monitors in metallic bags hang from the ceiling, approx 128 x 98 cms.

Regina Vater / Roberto Evangelista

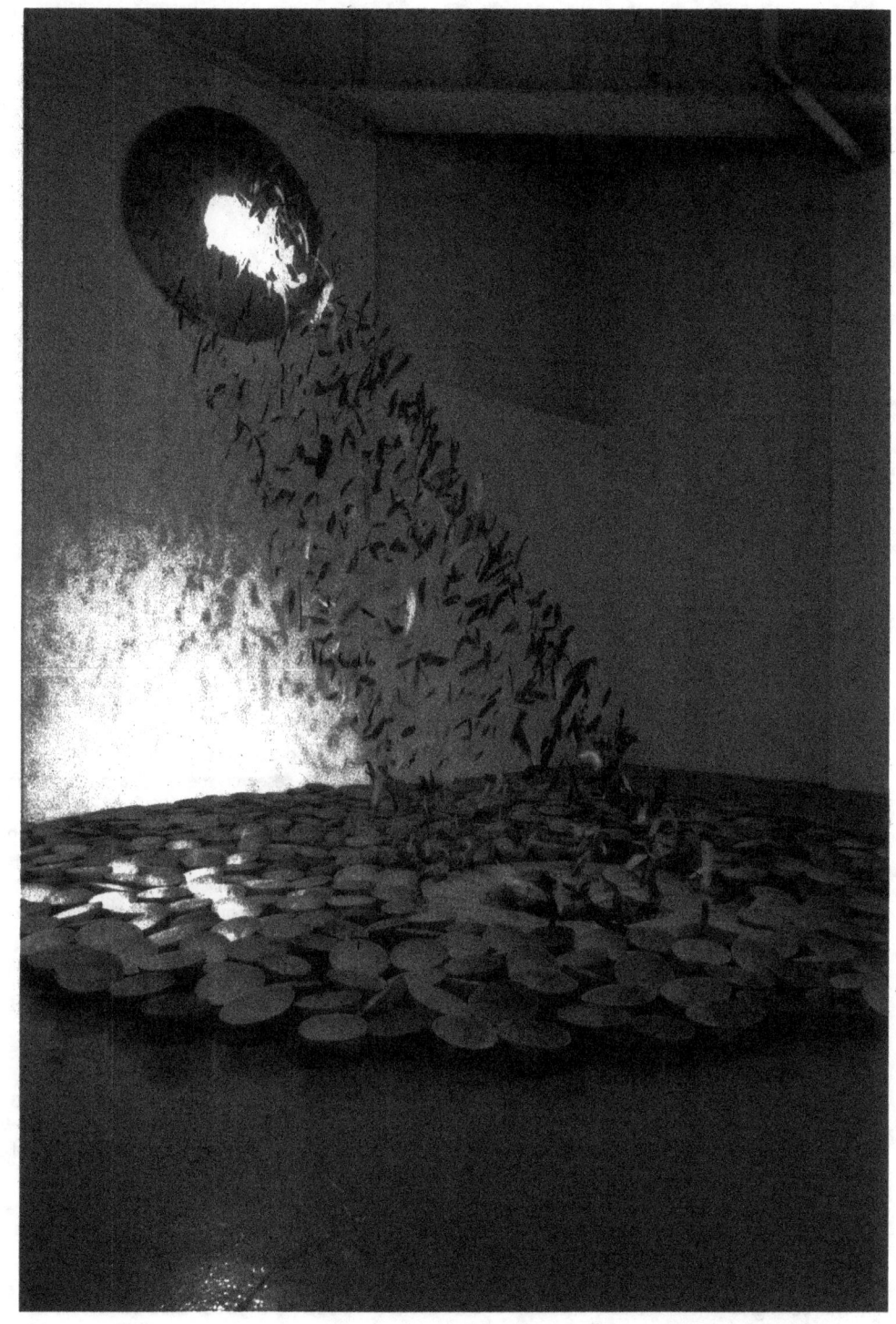

Nika Uiícana 1989.
Dedicated to Chico Mendes. 300 Amazonian gourds and several hundred
bird feathers. Installed at the Clocktower Gallery, New York.

I. My battle field is the memory of the essence.

Memory as being the record of the primordial forms: the circle, the square, the triangle.

The task: to record the first manifestations and their correlations: to research the enigma of their origin, as these figures have been - and always will be - present in all of Man's spatial conceptions.

Vital for these conceptions, essential to sight, the key to the enigma would reside in the way that man visualizes them and manipulates their symbolic charges. The Indian is the living link, closest to mythological dimensions, as his experience is concentrated in myths.

Their meanings and signifiers derive from an ancestral mythology; the prototypical figures remain there, untouchable in their original sense, as a living, spawning material, maintaining their original charges.

The method: decondition oneself, discard alien and alienating design and penetrate in order to reunite the links of lost memory.

And cleanse. Cleanse up to alpha, up to omega.

Up to the core.

II. In the Amazon, nature dominates and predominates.

And, despite massacres, the indigenous memory is still breathing. Some clearings remain untouched - there we can have access to sources. We live with drama. We learn from tragedy. The proposal is to recover primordial memory before the last sight.

III. He is the living link in the chain. The natural maker. Latent ancestral memory. With him, we can still learn to venerate the circle.

IV. The ecological shield, the reference point of a new archaic source, the reference point of a natural worldview. It is the awakening - rather late - to the discovery and reality of this dimension.

Roberto Evangelista

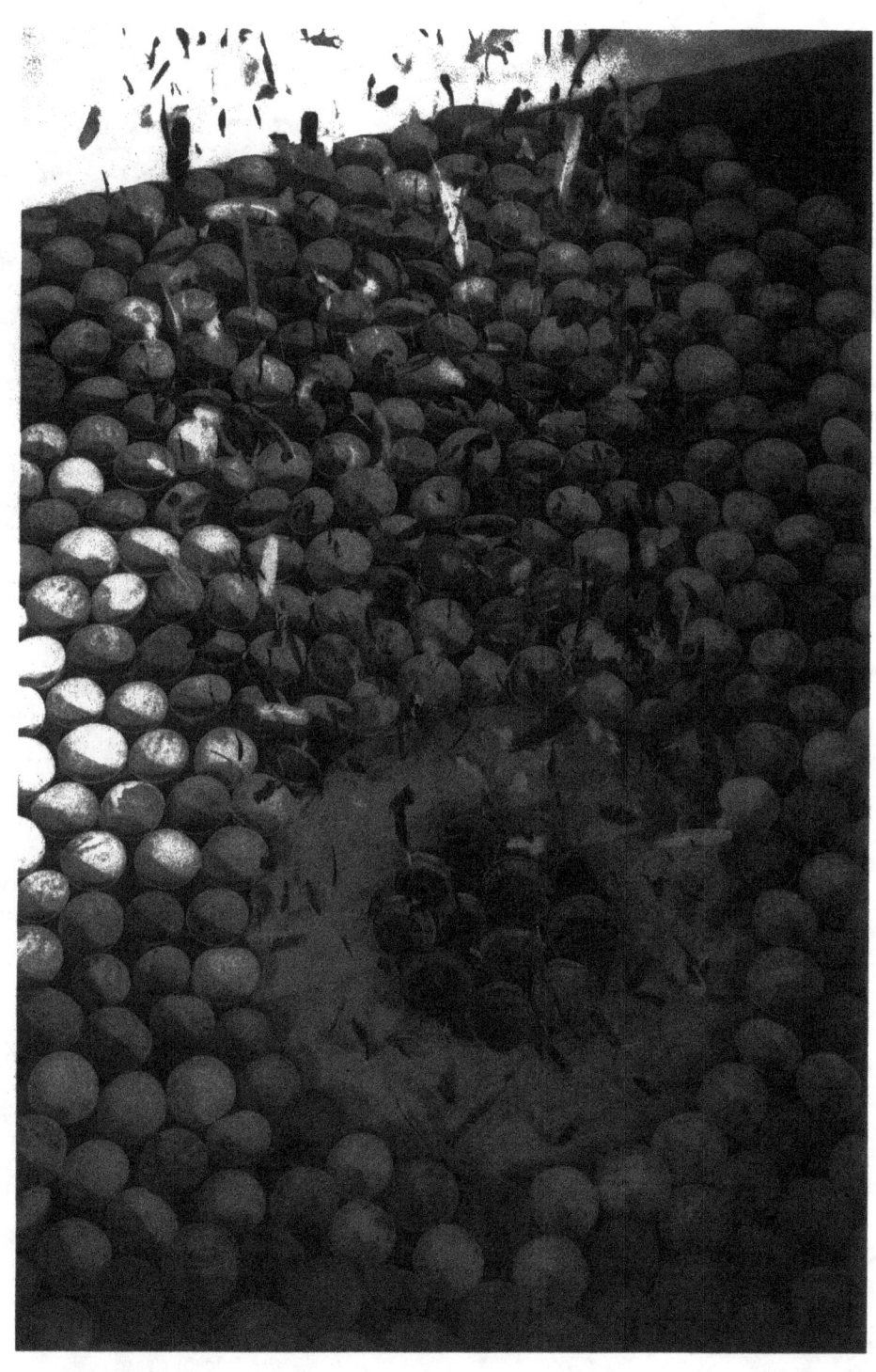

Nika Uiícana 1989,
dedicated to Chico Mendes. 300 Amazonian gourds and several hundred
bird feathers. Installed at the Clocktower Gallery, New York.

Roberto Evangelista

**Mater Dolorosa in Memoriam II
(On the Creation and Survival of forms)**

On a horizontal line, the remnants.
Father:
after the massacre, there remained only the scraps,
the streaks,
and residues of memory.
There
where we keep the words of the elders, to forget not
the beginning.
From mouth to ear,
for many moons,
the lines were passed on.
The information of the lines.
The formation of the lines.
The lines.
With them, without their knowing it,
we redesigned life and survived.

Our first fitting tools,
spawned from the sun and the water
Light or water, who was at the beginning?
The elders would say,
they were always together.
At the very beginning, well before the beginning,
Before the earth and the woods.
Before the first hut and the first clearing.

The elders would say:
in the beginning there never was chaos. And the
first one never slept.
Enormous eye. Bulging. Light of many eyes.
Floating. Circulating.
Circling.
Spawning circulations.
Circles in each eye.
Eye/Circle .
The first dwelling.
The Circle of nourishment. Pierced in the body.
The mysterious relations of spirit and stomach:
deep inside, the same form.
The Sun, high, high up.
And not leaving my body.
Thus,
water and air drew the unthinkable lines
and the Circle spawned all forms.

In the crossing of the sticks,
in the structure of the Uií,
big house,
the elders say, they took you prisoner.

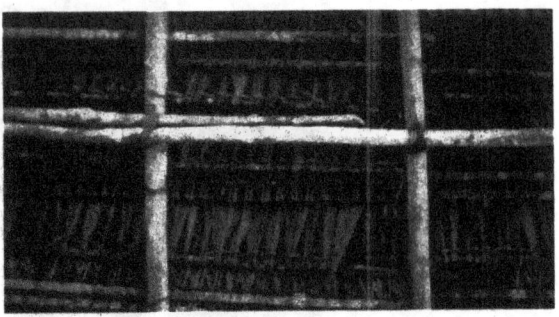

Still from the film **Mater Dolorosa in Memoriam II (on the Creation and Survival of Forms)**. Roof of 'OCA' (Indian communal house).

The loose, moving circle
was the only design the first ones
had to build the big shelter.
Nika Uiícana
every one shall stay in the same and be brothers.

And in the firm crossing of the sticks,
the elders say, they took you prisoner.
Since then you are present in all the doings and
undoings.
In all that is built.
Steady ropes and structures.
From the earth. From man.

Before, well before.
Between the circle and the square.
The spirit of man floated from the mystery
of the waters.
And inhabited the heads
and the heights.

Earth Mother: I decipher you.
    They devour you.
Earth Mother: I decipher you
    I devour you.
    And return to you.
    Until the consumption of the circles.
    Until the consumption of the circles.
    Until the consumption of the circles. . .

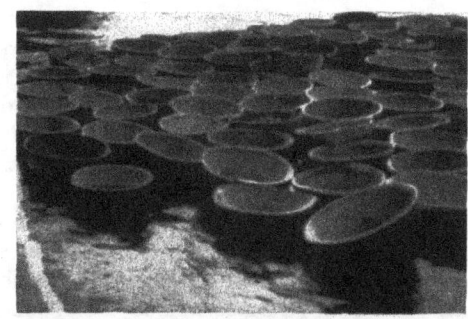

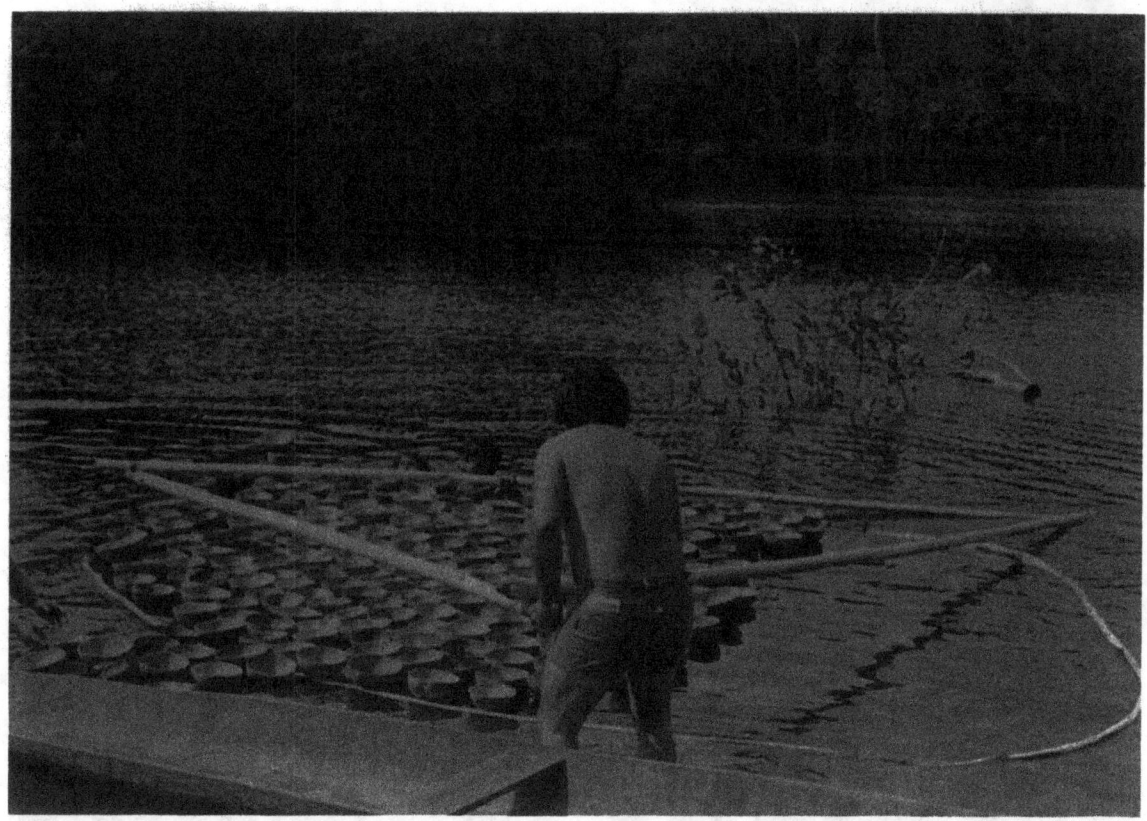

Floating installation on the Rio Negro. Stills from **Mater Doloroso In Memoriam II (on the Creation and Survival of Forms)**.

Nika Uiícana is a collaborative work by Regina Vater and Roberto Evangelista. It was originally commissioned by the Clocktower gallery in New York for an exhibition there in 1989, on the theme of 'artists' travels'. But Vater and Evangelista are also known as artists in their own right, each with their own distinctive work. It is important to establish this (they do after all live thousands of miles apart: Evangelista in Manaus, Amazonas, and Vater in Austin, Texas) before discussing the considerable concerns they have in common.

The issue of the fate of the rain forests, and the people who live in or near them, and especially the Amazon, has now reached blockbuster proportions in the West. It has generated an avalanche of books (from the coffee-table kind to specialised campaigning leaflets), TV programmes, cunning charity/advertising appeals, and generally given fresh stimulation to the international market of images. No one doubts its seriousness. But it is also an issue which raises in an acute and complex form the tension between the 'local' and the 'global' in the world today, and the influence of international power politics at every level of events. The promotion of an issue to 'global' proportions can very easily be used as a mask by the big powers to manipulate the situation to their advantage. For this reason Regina Vater, as a Brazilian artist resident in the United States, when putting forward proposals for her own work there, has felt it necessary to draw attention to an "obscure" side of an important international issue, namely, "the feelings of the Brazilian people on the subject".

Inside Brazil itself the issue of the local is important and quite complex too, since few Brazilians who live in the south have any direct experience of the Amazon as a region. A number of artists for a number of years have been preoccupied with ecological questions in Brazil. For some of them this has meant an intense involvement in the local: a specific place, history, people; and the

problematic of how to 'infect' the international, avant-garde discourse with this knowledge, this feeling, which for them is not local but 'central'. It has meant some kind of art/activism combination.

Roberto Evangelista was born in the Amazon and has always lived there. He studied philosophy at the University of Manaus. He has worked in theatre and film as well as the visual arts. His 'installations' have often used the method of a stark 'actualism' within specific contexts. For example, 14 years ago, in the midst of a large industrial exhibition held to celebrate the Zona Franca de Manaus, packed with glittering machines and electronic equipment of the multinational firms with an interest in 'transforming' the Amazon, he exhibited *Mater Dolorosa*. This consisted of a transparent acrylic box full of pieces of incinerated wood. It rested on a large square of fine white sand. Faced with such insane contradictions between richness and ruins (extremes implicating both nature and people), some artists have reached for the understatement, the ironic dislocation, the mixture of genres.

Regina Vater does so in her series of cibachrome prints, *Nature Morte*. Beautifully photographed in natural light, the allusion is to the Flemish tradition of still-life painting, where "dead animals were used as a reference to the abundance of nature" (and also, incidentally, to the patron's wealth). In Vater's series we see the left-overs of a macabre banquet, which is also the ruins of a European genre. In fact the allusion is not only to the 17th century but also to more recent genres. Fur or feather in a tea-cup, which for Surrealists like Meret Oppenheim signified the wild, untamed, the unconscious breaking into normality, in Vater's images can no longer stand for desire in the same way. They make us rethink the metaphor and its workings in our own psychology, while, it must be said, always retaining the beauty of the shaft of natural light.

The installation *Anakonda* (1989) by Regina Vater

mixes up several references and really invites the spectator to unravel them (spectators become incorporated in the piece via their reflections in the red plastic sheet against the wall). The video contains images of trees flashing past, and of intense traffic, intercut with the close-up of a turtle, which seems to be in agony (the turtle was the First Animal, according to Indian myths, and the broken pieces of its shell the source of all other animals). These images make the snake-skin rising on an earth mound, and the cut log, stand for the roads driven through the Amazon and the clearance of forest. The fact that the snake-skin is itself fake and made of plastic makes one unsure whether to read the reference to the snake as implying a treacherous or a subjugated energy.

Regina Vater is a multimedia artist, working in video, performance, installation, photography, visual poetry and artists' books. She has also been a pioneer curator of shows of experimental Latin American artists in the US. Many of her earlier works were conceptual devices for returning the institution 'art' to the sensory body and the cycles of nature. But along with the critical and deconstructive thread in her work, she has also, and especially in the collaborative installation with Roberto Evangelista, replied to the situation of crisis with an aesthetic of 'harmony'. *Nika Uiícana* means 'union of people' in Tucano, (one of the indigenous languages of Brazil). The notion of a homage to Chico Mendes (a leader of the Amazonian rubber-tappers union who was murdered by the order of a local landlord in 1988), is interpreted as a beautiful, peaceful, untroubled installation. Even feathers, normally in motion, become uncannily still. Vater and Evangelista have written of their aim to "recoup the beauty and energy of Brazil's indigenous past and the perpetual integration of that essential energy in the present". This desire may be felt in the material presence of the work: in a plenitude and generosity which is, however, conveyed with extreme

delicacy. A 'union' can also be found in the way the references and allusions to 'nature' and to 'culture' are pitched very closely together and become interdependent. The installation is a spatial device for making manifest a certain kind of energy between artist and spectator, using the 'universal' language of abstraction, rather than actual ritual references or forms.

A number of strands converge in the thoughts Roberto Evangelista has expressed about his work and about installations such as *Nika Uiícana*. First, an attachment to the modernist tradition of an economy and purity of means, which is linked with the idea of a universal visual language. The circle, square and triangle are "primordial" forms which he finds not only present but also "venerated" in the indigenous culture of the Indians of Brazil. The artist would only be able to give these forms their original "symbolic charges", for example, by tracing them back to the way they are handled in ancestral Indian mythologies and cultural practices:

....to record the first manifestations and their correlations: to research the enigma of their origins, as these figures have been - and always will be - present in all human spatial configurations.[22]

Nika Uiícana shows a kind of dualism or correlation: sky/earth-water (feathers, light-source/gourds), and the circular gourds unite several references: eating, drinking, and a reference to the crown of the head. Modernism was always closely and paradoxically associated with seeking origins, beginnings, and the *source* of energy. In Vater's and Evangelista's work this clearly has to do with the recovery of lost values in the present-day crisis of values. One way of treating the notion of the 'indigenous' is through purity of means and harmony. Another, and apparently opposite, is through the belief that there are no pure means. Whereas one tries to 'get close', tune in, and seeks the first-hand, the authentic, the whole, the essence; the other makes use of the debased, the completely mixed-up, the fragmentary, the second-hand - also, paradoxically, to get at the authentic. If the first approach is represented in this book by Regina Vater's and Roberto Evangelista's *Nika Uiícana*, the second is the territory of Juan Davila ∎

22. See Roberto Evangelista's statement, p. 96.

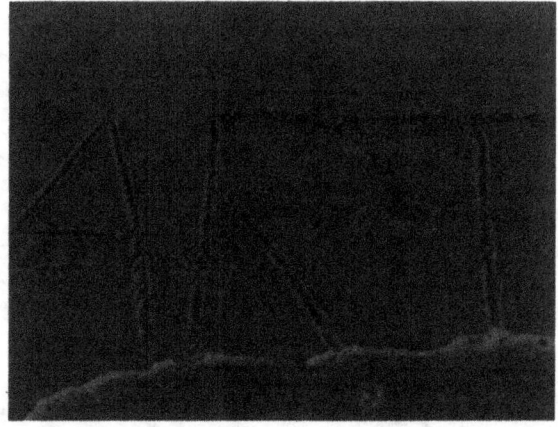

Regina Vater, stills from **Video Art** 1978,

Phillip Island, 27 Dec., 87

Dear Guy, I am writing to describe the paintings I intend to do for "Malas Artes".* They will be 3 canvases of 2 × 7 mt. each, that I intend to transport in a tube as luggage. Each painting will contain 3 scenes:

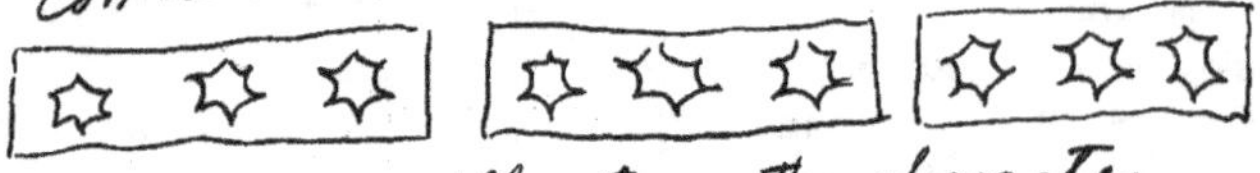

☆ ☆ ☆   ☆ ☆ ☆   ☆ ☆ ☆

The scenes will stage the character Juanito Laguna from Berni's popular engravings in Argentina. He will be a transvestite with a body as a simulacrum. I will dress him up in the make-up of the "exotic" Latin American styles of painting. I will cast him in the drawings done by Balthus of "Wuthering Heights" as Cathy. For example, 'Juanito Laguna's escape with Heathcliff to the moors' or 'Bitten by the Dog', etc. Juanito Laguna as a half-caste, mixed breed, arrives

2.

in the European "primal scene" of an english novel to enact the return of the outcast. He will be the 'Queen for a day' under an assumed name, a master of disguises (latin american collage) with nothing to hide (unlike the phallic mother he parodies) or to show. Collage and transvestism, the unreality of a copy, psychosis and hybridism, european debris are his borrowed femininity, his tools of the trade. He kisses Heathcliff in your class system scenario, the union of the weak, the counter-language of tyranny. Juanito Laguna says: "I have infinitely less reason to fear my neighbour's passions than your clause 28 injustice, for my neighbour's passions are contained by mine, whereas nothing stops or contains the injustices of your law."

yours sincerely,

Juan Davila

* Malas Artes was a previous title for *Transcontinental*.

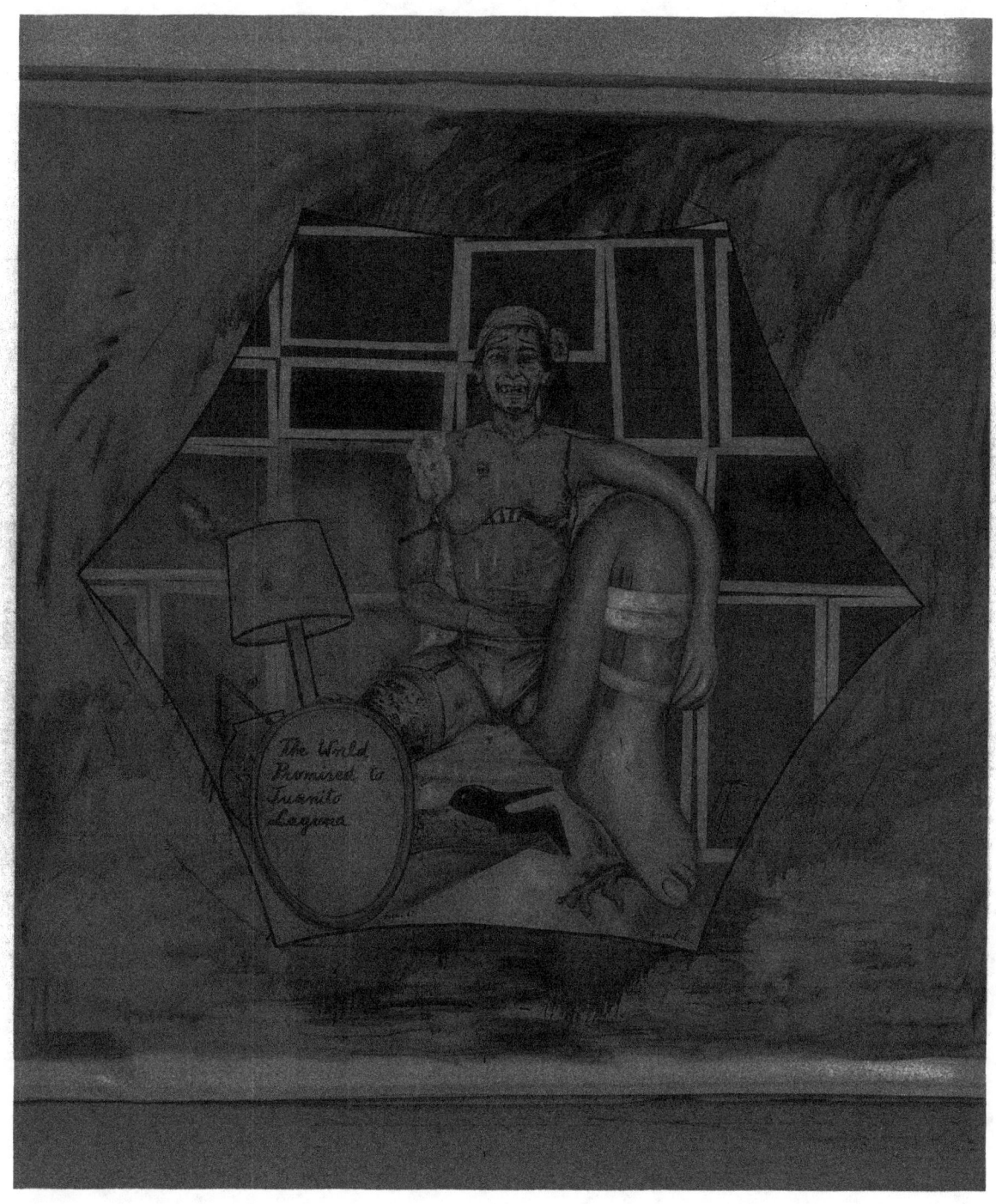

The World Promised to Juanito Laguna

Wuthering Heights *(Work in progress)* 1990, oil on canvas, in three parts 200X700 cms each.

Pages 100-105: letters, fragments and early stages of the work which was painted
specially for the *Transcontinental* exhibition, December 1989 - January 1990.

Melbourne, 19 Jan., 80

Dear Guy, I am painting now and enclose photographs of some fragments.

2 mt. 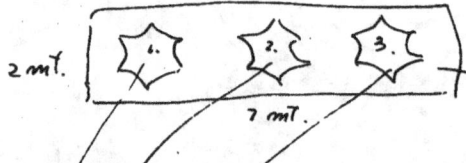 L.S. Lowry academic landscape

7 mt.

medallions with the illustrations of Wuthering Heights

1. The World Promised to Juanito Laguna
2. Heathcliff and Juanito Laguna on the Moor (chapter 6)
3. The Birth of Juanito Laguna 'you needn't have touched me'(chapter 7) etc.

All latin american references I will use can be found in the english censorship publication art in latin america, the Modern Era, 1820 – 1980 The Hayward Gallery, London.

Yours sincerely,

Juan Davila

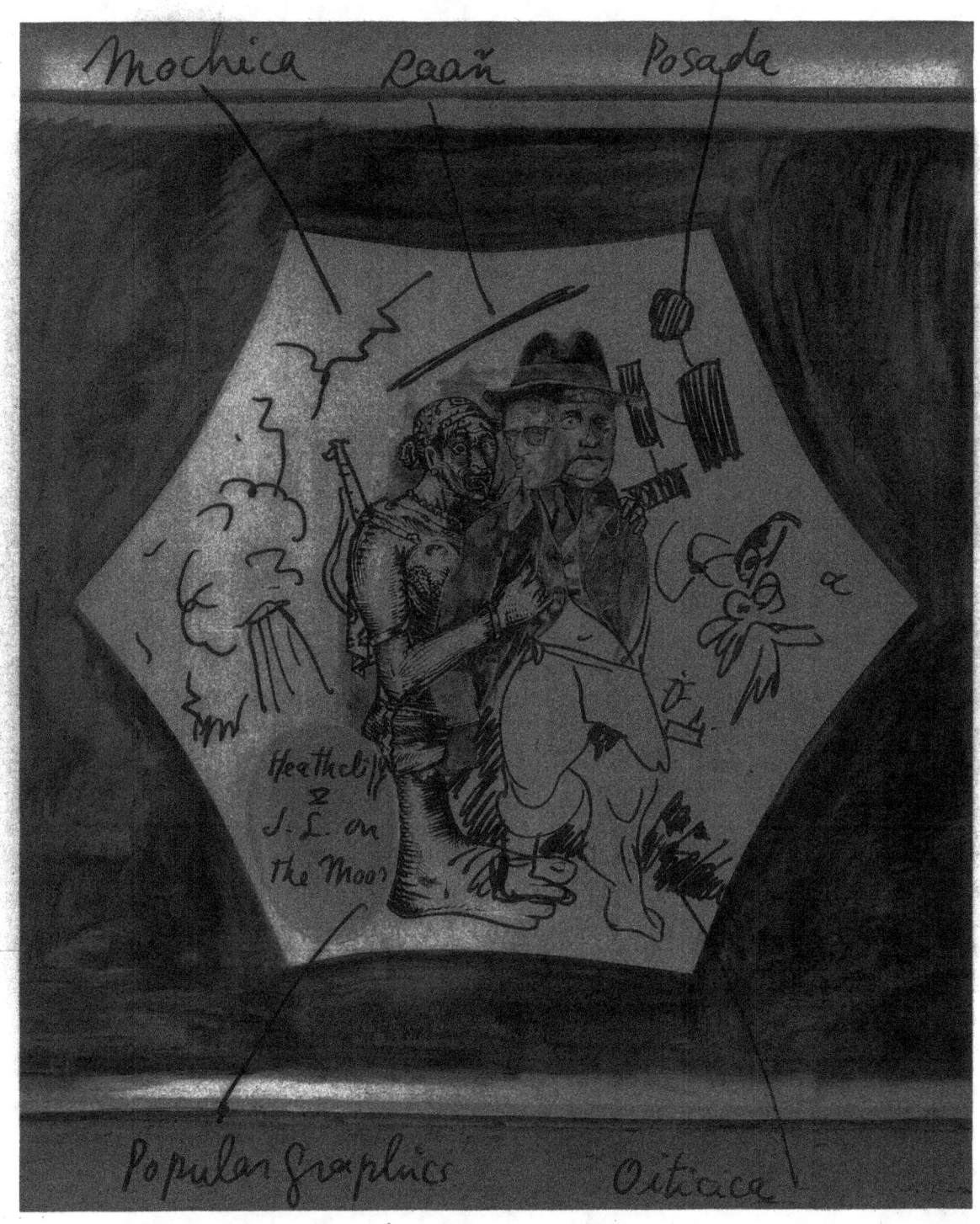

Wuthering Heights (Work in progress).

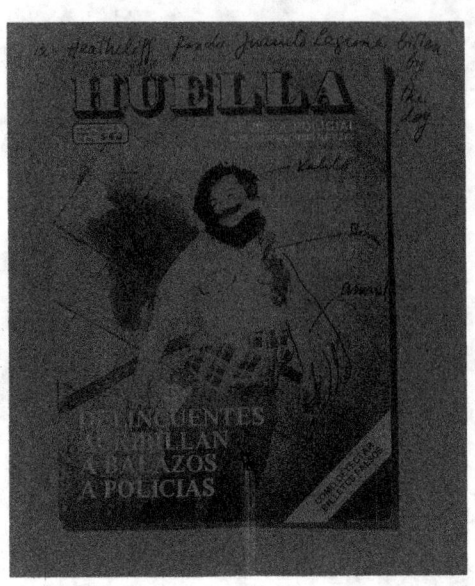

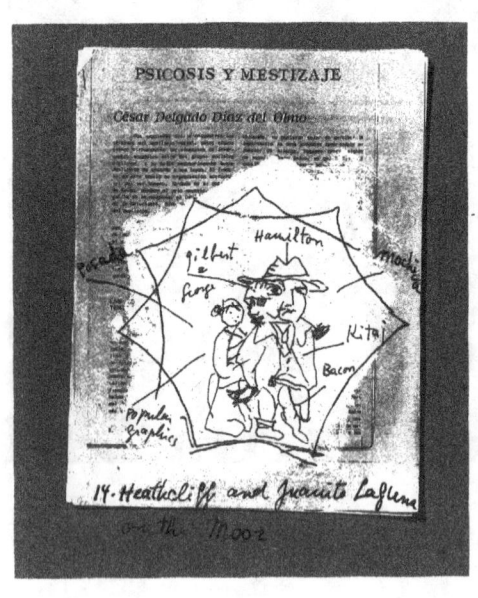

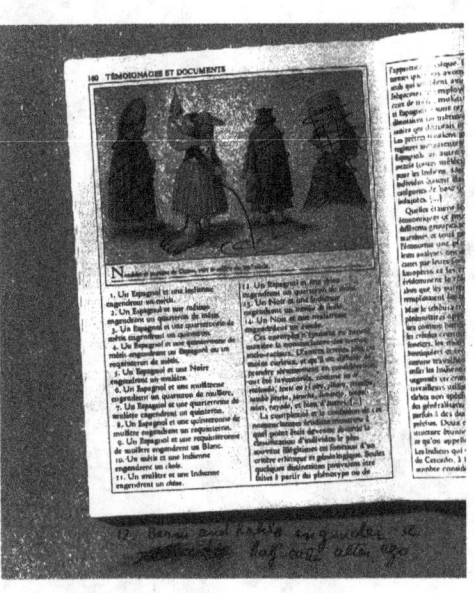

Wuthering Heights *(Work in progress).*

Melbourne, 30 January, 1990.

Guy Brett
38 Archbishops Place
London SW2 2AJ
ENGLAND

Dear Guy,

In the invitation to this exhibition you mention as a reference the atmosphere created by the large art-historical exhibition shown last year at the Hayward Gallery in London. In my opinion that exhibition is a good example of a dominant view. Latin America appears there as exotic, primitive, quaint, pure. That is expressed by the erasure of all national art histories turning the continent into one place, by applying to the cultural material classifications of periods and genres that originate in the European sense of history and also by using a concept of time and space that is unitarian. Thus the exhibition brings to the English shore a remnant of your 18th and 19th century hegemonic thinking by which the world and societies were conceived according to the needs of power with rationality as its tool. Latin America in that schema shows a failed 'modernisation' where the battles against despotism, social unequality and servitude became the 'great narratives' of history, the impossibility of Latin American utopian thought. At the Hayward exhibition that continent undergoes a similar metamorphosis: it is now a culture without seams or violence, a place without a voice—no discourse generated there is offered—and because the show is a sort of historical compendium, a place without a present (recent art is not included); a mere reproduction of dependence.

Latin America is not a constituted culture around a clear nucleus of identity where cultural materials are sedimented; its technical rationality is different to the European one, its imaginery life is *dual* (outside the modern versus non-modern dichotomy) and its links between history and time differ in the sense that it has a sequential and simultaneous time (Anibal Quijano). Arguedas' utopian solution seems relavent in this context: to use the dominant language in order to convey the voice of Latin America rearticulating both cultural heritages. If the actual exhibition was to be used as a right of reply, one could attempt to frustrate the expectations of what Latin American art is today, rather than try to engage in the present First World modernity crisis by placing oneself in the rôle of 'other' that is expected: the safe Academy of the marginal, the indigenous, the Third World, the provincial, etc. Access is not a product of cultural domination but it can be one of its mechanisms. How can one avoid bringing to the European market new products? Latin America can be a dominant subculture in the dominant culture, a pleasing product—as the Hayward exhibition demonstrates—for the old demand.

Yours Sincerely,

Juan Davila

The first appearance of Juan Davila's paintings in Britain will surely be in one way a 'reply'. His paintings will refuse to be made the stuff of romantic projections about Latin America on the one hand, and on the other they will assume the right to know and define aspects of English culture, a reversal of the traditional relationship. But it is very likely that this will be only a part of what they will do. They will expose these ancient antagonisms and power struggles, not in terms of secure and separate identities but in terms of cross-breedings, cross-infections and mixings, touching on intimate taboos and repressions. Very likely these clashes and amalgams will be enacted in scenes which are both shockingly carnal and extremely sophisticated and ironic in their play with every kind of contemporary visual code.

"I am interested in the process of replacement of what is real by its reproduction", Juan Davila has said.[21] His words indicate not only the scope of the enquiry he has made in his work over the last fifteen years into the complex workings of mediation, but also hint that this enquiry will be a way of getting closer to what is 'real', which the reproduction replaces.[23] A critical concern with *reproduction* necessarily entails a concern with artistic *production*, and its material conditions, since the two processes are so intimately connected. Davila's paintings lay their visual devices and codes open to view; in fact they open themselves to the contemporary conditions of visual production and reproduction in the least idealized way possible. Davila's 'quotes' range from the sacrosanct field of art (taking in our consumption of our 'own' culture, and our discovery of novelties) to mass culture: media images, comics, pornography. All are contained today within a global market of images, even the artist's own inventory and analysis, a fact Davila wittily acknowledges by often marking his picture surface with a blatant or discreet bar-code or colour-scale (as if already preparing it for reproduction in art magazines).

Davila's candid view of the way the 'system' works could be connected with his own biography and position as an 'outsider': "The circumstance of living in two extremes of the world", Davila has said, "in two peripheral cultures (*i.e. those of Chile, his country of origin, and of Australia where he has lived since 1974*), slowly forced me to look at the materiality of the circumstances where art works operate. It also forced me to assume the dimensions of the loss of language and history that emigrants have, to find options for identity."[24] In his brilliant essay on the artist's work, the Peruvian critic Gustavo Buntinx compared Davila's position with that of the passer-by, the wanderer in great cities, the type of modern subject identified by Baudelaire in the 19th century, except that the conditions have changed:

Davila's is also the gaze of the passer-by, but in an expanded and contemporary dimension. His object has never been the urban turmoil - already an antiquated experience - but the enthralling flicker of the mass media and the new visuality they bring into being: transnational, saturating, indiscriminate.[25]

Despite his openness, Davila is far from being a mere witness of this new visuality. Despite the critical exactitude with which he assembles what are drily called 'codes', they never meet in his paintings with academic detachment or decorative prettiness. They clash violently. Their meetings and hybridizations are either a corrosive irritant, a clumsy graft ("like bad cooking", Davila has described it), or libidinously erotic, or both (in fact the multiple nature of these clashings and mixings is reduced by any sequential description). In one sense Davila's paintings continue a very old tradition, that of making travesties of or 'debasing' established ideas (and visual codes) to the level of the body and its functions (the tradition of the grotesque, satire, carnival, abuse and laughter, which Mikhail Bakhtin once described as a "boundless ocean...in the midst of [which] the bodily canons of art, belles lettres, and polite conversation of modern times is a tiny island").[26] But they banish any nostalgia in this relationship by giving a new inflection to the word 'travesty': that this body, and all its attributes, including its clothing, is transvestite.

Replying to the inevitable questions about his relationship to the recent history of Chile, Davila has said that, for him, the question of sexual repression is as important as political repression and has tended to be ignored in the rhetoric of liberation.[27] He has points in common with the area which the novelist Manuel Puig explored in the meeting of his two characters in *Kiss of the Spider Woman*. In fact this whole question of sexuality, and sexual identity, is being explored with tremendous pertinence and audacity by a number of Latin American writers and artists today, a piquant fact considering the often-mentioned traditions of *machismo* in Latin America, and the repressed undertones of sexuality in Catholicism. The Mexican writer and performer Jesusa Rodriguez, speaking on TV recently of her play *Council of Love*, a work which mixes these two areas of sexuality and religion brilliantly—speaking through the mask of her own androgynous make-up reflected in her dressing-room mirror—referred to the burden of traditional sexual roles and stereotypes and the 'obsolete' identities they offer.[28] Nelly Richard, writing about the exhibition *Adam's Apple* (photographs by Paz Errázuriz of Chilean transvestites, combined with their words collected by Claudia Donoso), recently made a telling contrast between the world of the transvestites and the world of the military regime, as it concerned attitudes to the body.[29]

Davila's paintings are often considered particularly

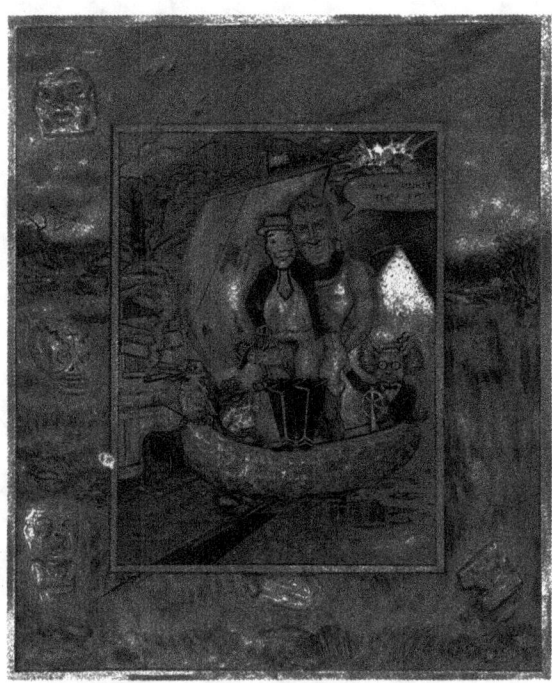

Utopia (detail), oil and collage on canvas, 180 x 1050 cms.

shocking because they speak of these matters through charged figures of pornographic illustration, rather than the "idealized, humanistic"[30] tradition of the nude in painting. As Gustavo Buntinx has pointed out, Davila's works have been attacked in terms very similar to those used against Manet's paintings *Olympia* and *Déjeuner sur l'Herbe* in 19th century France, because, in his view, Davila has again introduced "the evidence of the present into the mythological order of artistic representation".[31] The erotic brings outraged reaction, but actually Davila's paintings defeat simple readings. They are extremely dense (aside from the thematic of the body, there is also one of domestic life and everyday objects which uses the impurities and incongruities of kitsch to construct its own ironic meanings). They have such a complexity of parodying that it is hard to find a borderline between the process of affirming and negating.

More recent paintings, however, concern themselves with a power struggle. They can be seen as a translation of the persistent inequalities of the world and the histories of colonialism into the era of the 'global market of images', drawing battle-lines in the complexity and confusion of transnational communications. In some paintings, an 'ornamental' border stands for the 'periphery', surrounding the 'centre of power'. But it is hardly as simple as that: impurity enters both scenes, necessarily, since Davila has declared his intention to

work "not by idealistic representations, but by exposing the materiality of the signs of culture".[32] One of his starting-points today is, as Buntinx describes

> ...that local painting (for example, Frida Kahlo, the Mexican muralists or Fernando Botero) which enters successfully into the international market, offering a parody of the mythical image of Latin America. Parody of a parody, pictorial quote of a cultural quote, these recent works of Davila drastically confound the stereotypes of our identity. At the same time, however, they attain a sincere approximation to what is popular and particular in Latin American experience.[33]

Wuthering Heights, the work painted for the exhibition in Manchester, will very likely continue this power struggle, with Juanito Laguna as a kind of popular, multiple, trickster figure whose survival in different, 'quoted', mediated, simultaneous worlds, is connected with his/her transvestism, with overcoming the "monological voice"[34] ∎

22. "A Question of im-pertinence", interview between Juan Davila and Paul Foss, *Hysterical Tears: Juan Davila*, London GMP, 1985, p.10.

23. For a beautiful and subtle visual statement on mediation and re-framing, and the ambiguities between the real and the reproduction, see Philip Pocock's colour photographs of decaying Lower East Side murals in New York in *The Obvious Illusion*, New York; George Braziller, 1980. The context is different, and Pocock's approach is one of the delight rather than critique, making the comparison with Davila very interesting.

24. Interview between Juan Davila and Paul Foss, op. cit., p.11

25. Gustavo Buntinx, "Vi(r)ajes", in *El Fulgor de lo Obsceno*, Santiago de Chile: Francisco Zegers Editor, 1989, p.15.

26. Mikhail Bakhtin, *Rabelais and His World*, Bloomington: Indiana University Press, 1984, p.319.

27. See interview between Juan Davila and Paul Foss, op. cit.

28. Jesusa Rodriguez speaking in the film *Love and Power* (dir. Rossana Horsley), Channel Four, 5 December 1989.

29. "In the case of the military, training and torture are the techniques used to force the body to comply with norms or to regret having transgressed them, either by setting the body up as a model of rectitude, or by punishing it... At the other extreme of the corporal repetoire of learning and initiation, the transvestite reconstructs his/her appearance to become a parody of the order in which the correspondence between sex and gender are established" - preface by Nelly Richard to *Adam's Apple: Chile - Transvestites*, photographs by Paz Errazuriz, text by Claudia Donoso, Australian Centre for Photography, Paddington NSW, Oct- Nov 1989.

30. Interview between Juan Davila and Paul Foss, op. cit., p.12

31. Gustavo Buntinx, op cit., p.20

32. Interview between Juan Davila and Paul Foss, op. cit., p.15

33. Gustavo Buntinx, op cit., p.35.

34. Interview between Juan Davila and Paul Foss, op. cit., p.14

Second Skin

The play of 'insincerity' and 'inauthenticity' is a tried tactic for getting at the truth in the face of official values. Oscar Wilde used it, as an Irish, emigré, homosexual writer in Victorian London. In fact many of Wilde's witticisms are based precisely on reversing the 'straight', the commonplace wisdom:

> Man is seldom himself when he talks in his own person. Give him a mask, and he will tell you the the truth. (*The Artist as Critic*)

Each artist's work recorded here represents in one way or another the breaking down of the protocols of art and of monolithic, simple, unitary selves and identities. Juan Davila has pointed to the employment of this tactic in Latin American history in the perpetual creation of hybrids and syncretisms: "You take something from yourself, something from the conqueror"; and he has suggested as a mythical precedent or parallel the figure of Xipe Totec, the Mexican god who wore a second skin over his own.[1]

This connection suddenly reminded me of watching, by chance, a soft-drink commercial on Chilean television in 1986. The routine unwound in a stereotypical Western saloon, but one saw that it was populated by many of Chile's leading actors and actresses, including one I knew well as an exile in London, who played the bartender. These were people who had received death-threats, who play commercials in order to survive, commercials made by directors who, in Chile, lend out their equipment after hours for the use of independent film and video makers. Knowing all this made one view the manipulative charade of consumerism, and the powers which stand behind it, in a highly sardonic light.

1. In a conversation with the writer, London, May 1989.

Biographies

Waltercio Caldas, b. 1946, Rio de Janeiro, Brazil.
Lives Rio de Janeiro.

Juan Davila, b. 1946, Santiago de Chile.
Lives Melbourne, Australia.

Eugenio Dittborn, b. 1943, Santiago de Chile.
Lives Santiago de Chile.

Roberto Evangelista, b. 1946, Manaus, Amazonas, Brazil.
Lives Manaus.

Victor Grippo, b. 1936, Junin, Buenos Aires, Argentina.
Lives Buenos Aires.

Jac Leirner, b. 1961, São Paulo, Brazil.
Lives São Paulo.

Cildo Meireles, b. 1948, Rio de Janeiro, Brazil.
Lives Rio de Janeiro.

Tunga, b. 1952, Palmares, Pernambuco, Brazil.
Lives Rio de Janeiro.

Regina Vater, b. 1943, Rio de Janeiro, Brazil.
Lives Austin, Texas, USA.

TRANSCONTINENTAL

Nine Latin American Artists
Written and compiled by Guy Brett
Edited by Elizabeth A. Macgregor

This publication accompanies the exhibition curated by Guy Brett in collaboration with Ikon Gallery, Birmingham and Cornerhouse, Manchester, 24 March - 28 April 1990. The project could not have been realised without the active involvement of all the artists. Their cooperation is deeply appreciated.

Collections

Jac Leirner: André L' Huillier, Geneva
                Joseph Farine, Galerie Andata/Ritorno, Geneva
                Luiz Buarque de Hollanda, Rio de Janeiro
Victor Grippo: Jorge and Marion Helft, Buenos Aires

Acknowledgements

With financial assistance from the Arts Council of Great Britain and its International Initiatives Fund, Visiting Arts, the Henry Moore Foundation, and Empresa de Navegação Aliança S/A Shipping Company.

Special thanks to the following:
The British Council, Rio de Janeiro; Clocktower, Institute of Contemporary Art, New York City; Carlos Afonso Silva Campos; Moises Spitz; Afonso Costa; Malcolm Imrie; Lucia Noguiera; John Ray, Twycross Zoo; Varig, Brazilian Airlines.

The making of *Godard Sculpture* by Waltercio Caldas was sponsored by Holvoet NV, Kortrijk - Heule, Belgium and produced by Kanaal Art Foundation, Kortrijk, Belgium.

Parts of the texts on Tunga and Cildo Meireles originally appeared in catalogues published by the Kanaal Art Foundation, Kortrijk and the Whitechapel Art Gallery, London; parts of the text on Eugenio Dittborn in the catalogue of his exhibition at the Australian Centre for Photography 1989.

Photographic Credits

pp.41, 44, 45 Wilton Montenegro, pp.42, 43 Pedro Oswaldo Cruz, pp.64, 67 Romulo Fialdini, pp.24, 65, 68 Cesar Caldas, p.69 Sergio Zalis, pp.70, 71 Rio Branco, pp.73, 74, 75, 76, 77, 111 Jorge Brantmeyer, pp.32, 93 Ari Macropolous, pp.29, 48, 49, 52 Gilles Hutchinson, pp.20, 53, 95 Guy Brett.

Ikon Gallery
58-72 John Bright Street,
Birmingham B1 1BN.
Tel 021 643 0708.

Cornerhouse
70 Oxford Street,
Manchester M1 5NH.
Tel 061 228 7621.

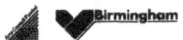

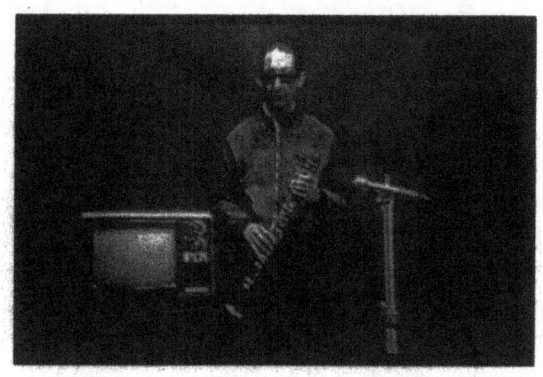

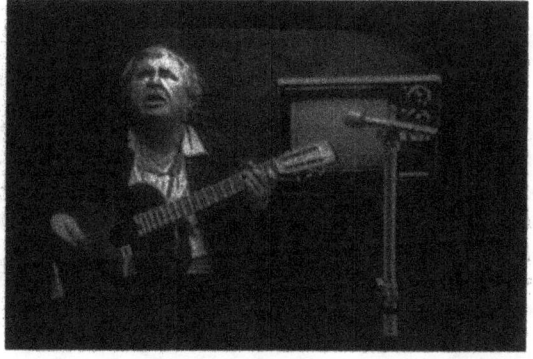

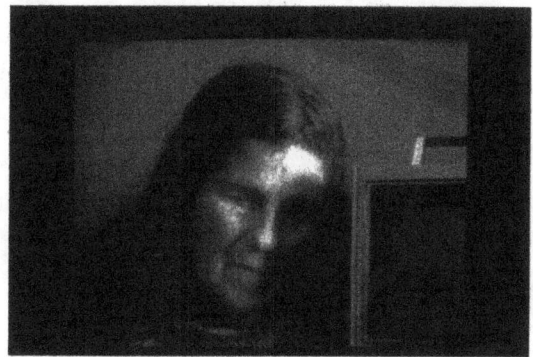

Eugenio Dittborn, **Five Preparatory Sketches for a History of Music** 1986. Video, 34 minutes, in colour. The photos show blind street musicians and a street clarinetist, also blind, all of whom work daily in the streets of central Santiago de Chile.

www.ingramcontent.com/pod-product-compliance
Lightning Source LLC
Chambersburg PA
CBHW081006170526
45158CB00010B/2925